GIFT *of the* PAST

Nellie Reynolds

Previous books,
Rafting With Grandmother
Grandmother's Adventure

Co-Author
High Mileage Hearts

iUniverse, Inc.
Bloomington

Gift of the Past

iUniverse books may be ordered through booksellers or by contacting:

iUniverse
1663 Liberty Drive
Bloomington, IN 47403
www.iuniverse.com
1-800-Authors (1-800-288-4677)

ISBN: 978-1-4502-9097-5 (pbk)
ISBN: 978-1-4502-9101-9 (ebk)

Printed in the United States of America

iUniverse rev. date: 1/14/2011

Dedicated to past and future generations.

Special thanks to

Jack Colglazier
Gordon Reynolds
Barbara Reynolds
Randy Reynolds
Andy Reynolds
Alex Reynolds
Tara Croy
Shannon Tompkins
Barry Powell

Preface

I am writing this book with the thought that maybe some day a person will be interested in knowing how life was in the Nineteenth and Twentieth Century. I have been blessed by having stories written by my grandparents in the Eighteen Hundreds. There are poems written by my granddad, Webster Baker, when he left Indiana to go with his parents for Kansas to homestead. One poem is about the girl he had to leave behind, that girl was Maggie Chess, my grandmother. These writings are very precious to me. There are stories of the early Nineteen Hundreds and how life was on the farm near what is now Spring Mill State Park in Indiana.

Many of the stories about Mitchell, Indiana came from Jack Colglazier, my cousin, things he remembered as a little boy growing up in Mitchell in the 1920s and early 1930s. He had two boy cousins of almost the same age. The three cousins had a wonderful time teasing their Granddad, Jake Colglazier.

The early married years of my dad, Chester Baker and my mother, Louisa Colglazier Baker, hold many memories, as there was no running water nor electricity.

Life in Mitchell, Indiana when my dad and my mother's brother, Clay Colglazier, owned a car garage and filling station in late 1920's was very different from what it is today in 2010.

Some of the stories are about my teen years growing up in Bedford, Indiana. Then the book goes on to my married life and the birth of my two sons. With life comes death. My husband died at the age of 52.

I was the Food Director for Warren Township Schools in Indianapolis, Indiana for twenty six years.

My life as an airplane pilot was very different and special for me. I was very fortunate to experience many wonders that God allowed me to have.

I have been blessed with a wonderful family and my grandchildren have played a big part in my life. Two former books, "Rafting with Grandmother" and "Grandmother's Adventures", tell of the joy I have had with my wonderful grandchildren. There is also a book called "High Mileage Hearts' co-authored with eight other people that has many memories.

May future generations look back and enjoy these experiences.

There are stories of the Chess, Baker, Colglazier and Reynolds family.

Contents

Part One:
MAGGIE AND WEBSTER

Chapter 1 —
Webster Washington Baker

WEBSTER WAS BORN DURING the turmoil of the Civil War on April 20, 1862. He already had one sister, Charlotte, born the year before. There were ten children born to the union of John Newton Baker and Sarah Ellen Porter Baker, four daughters and six sons. All of them were born in Washington or Lawrence County, Indiana. The last child was Oliver Otto Baker born June 5, 1884.

Tragedy struck March 5, 1879 in Lawrence County. Arthur Baker, age six months was in his mother's arms while she was seated on the front seat of a wagon. A branch was caught on the Oxen harness and snapped loose. It struck the child and he was killed.

In Abraham Lincoln's second Inaugural Address on March 4, 1865, he said "but one of them would make war rather than let the nation survive, and the other would accept war rather than let it perish, and the war came."

In 1862 the Homestead Act was passed by Congress; under this act, any head of a family, or any adult who had not bore arms against the government could become owner of 160 acres of public land. All he had to do was to live on it for five years and cultivate it.

In 1885 John Newton Baker gathered his family together and moved to Kansas. They took with them their eight remaining children ranging from age one year to twenty-five years of age. They followed the Santa Fe Trail till they got to Missouri. Since most wagon trains camped overnight by rivers and streams that were prone to flash flooding, the pioneers always had a flood story or two to tell. The Baker ladies slept in the wagon while the men folk bedded down under it. The rains came and the suddenly drenched boys harnessed the teams and pulled the wagons to higher ground.

They arrived in Harper Co. Kansas some time before December of 1885.They spent time there perhaps because of the weather. At that time their son Granville was married to a girl that was on the wagon train.

In 1886 with Granville and his new bride they continued on to their Homestead claim on the Great Plains in Grant Co, Kansas. In order to own the land they must stay on it for five years and work the property. Each of the adult boys had their own land to homestead. Once there they constructed a sod house. John Newton was reported to be a school teacher and he also built a sod school house next to his home. Two of his daughters also became school teachers.

Here is a description of how to make a sod house from the book," making a Modern America". The first step in making a sod house was to plow a strip of thick sod with a moldboard plow. With a spade, the upturned sod was cut into bricks about three feet long. Then the sod bricks were laid in place and held together with adobe mud (this is a mixture of earth, water and grass or straw). To make walls, door frames and window frames were set in the walls. In the best sod houses, roofs were made of wood rafters, covered with boards, tarpaper, and a layer if sod over all. In a short time, weed and grass and even sunflowers would flourish on the roof.

One evening Webster returned home late. He was tired, and there was no need to light a lamp to get into bed, Webster laid down, and soon realized he was not alone, He heard a sound and jumped up. The sound was made by a rattlesnake, which struck at him. The snake did not break the skin, but got tangled up in his bed shirt. Webster jumped out of bed, and ran outdoors. The rattler finally fell off out side in the open. It was a very close brush with possible death.

Sara Ellen was remembered as a sturdy woman with a rare sense of humor. She was an excellent seamstress and cared about the appearance of her family even on the dust ridden plains of her home. Sara's hair was always yellow because she rubbed it with lye soap to keep it in place.

Webster was a young man of twenty-three when his family moved to Kansas. He left behind his sweetheart, a young girl of 18 years of age. Here is his poem to that young girl named Maggie Chess

Separation

1st With all my soul lets part
      Since both seem anxious to be free
      I'll send you home your heart
      If you will send mine back to me

2nd We've had some happy times together
      But joys most often change the wind
      And spring would be but gloomy weather
      If we had nothing else but spring.

3rd If you think best we'll break the grove
      If you think better we'll be free
      I would not hold for all the world
      A heart that has no love for me!

4th If you are tired of the heart
      That you have taught to love none else but you
      When you can love another one
      I'll try to love another too.

5th Farewell! And may some future lover
      Soon claim this heart that I resign,
      And with exultant joys discover
      The charms that once were mine!

      Webster W. Baker
      App?????????
      Grant County
      Kansas

Webster with his brother, Granville and Grandville's new bride, also named Maggie, returned to Indiana some time between 1888 and 1890. There he married his childhood sweetheart, Maggie Chess, on Feb. 7, 1892. He would have been thirty and she would have been twenty-five.

Indian Maiden

1st As I was walking for pleasure one day,
To seek recreation I scarcely could say,
As I sat amusing myself in the shade,
Oh who would come near me but a young Indian maid.
She said down beside of me and took hold of my hand.
Saying "You look like a stranger though none of my band.
And if you will terry you're welcome to come,
And cheer with myself in a snug little home."

2nd Together we wonder, together did go
Till we came to the log hut where the coconuts grow.
This young maiden was fair and was kind
And played her part well like the heaven's ?????
One Monday morning, one morning in May
Her heart it bled sorely unto her I did say.
"I'm going away to leave you so fare you well a???????
My ship set for toward home I did steer"

3rd The last time I saw her,
She stood on the strand
And as I passed by her she waved her small hand.
Saying, "When you get over to the girl that you love
Just think of little Myauhee in the coconut grove"
And now I'm safe landed on my old native shore
MY friends and companions gather round me once more
I look all around me but none do I see
That I can compare with the little Myauhee.

Chapter 2 —
The Chess Family

THE CHESS FAMILY CAME from England to Virginia in the seventeen hundreds. They migrated from Virginia through Kentucky and Ohio as they made their way to Indiana and Illinois.

One of the Chess boys married an Indian maiden from the Shawnee tribe near Fort Pitt, Pennsylvania.

James Chess Senior was born in 1777 in Pennsylvania. He died in 1839 or 1843 in Cessna Park, Illinois. He was married to Pricilla Roberts who was the sister to Bishop Roberts of the Methodist Church. Rivervale Church camp is named after Bishop Roberts.

James Chess Jr. was born June 15, 1811 in Kentucky. He married Margaret Ellen Matthew. He died June 10, 1879 in Lawrence County. He is buried in Lawrenceport Cemetery.

James Wesley Chess was born in August 29, 1836 in Bono, Lawrence County, Indiana. He married Julia A. (Fellows) Andrews. Julia had previously been married to a man by the name of Andrews. She had a daughter by the name of Velvina Andrews. She was born Sept 26, 1860. She married W. H. Brooking. The Musical Organ I, Nellie Reynolds, donated to Spring Mill State Park was given to Velvina by her stepfather, James Chess.

James and Julie had six children, two girls and four boys. They were:

1. Margaret ((Maggie) Jane Chess born Nov. 9, 1867 –died 1930. She married Webster Washington Baker on Feb.7 1892

2. Henry Howard Chess born April 30 1869. He married Florence Hughes

3. Amanda Ellen Chess She married Albert Hall. They had one child, Alberta who married Lester Lowery. They had no children.

4. Wesley Edward Chess, born Nov. 2, 1872. He died 1938. Married Emma McCullough.

5. Albert Burk Chess, born Jan 12 1874. Married to Melinda Mathews Feb.12.1902. They went west to California.

6. Charles Elmer Chess was born April 5, 1878. He was married to Gertrude Burton, she was born in 1882 and died in 1901 during childbirth. She is buried in Burton Cemetery in Mitchell, Indiana. Charles later moved to California and remarried.

Maggie was my grandmother. She was very special to me. As a young girl she had a vivid imagination and the desire to write a journal .Her journal is dated 1886.She would have been 19 years old. Her story of "Flying to the Moon' was years ahead of her time. She wrote of her brother, Howard, attending the commencement exercise at Southern Indiana Normal College in Mitchell. She and the family would walk to church in Mitchell, four miles, on Sunday and take their lunch and spend the day. Sunday school would be in the evening. They went to the Church of Christ on the east side of Mitchell. The road to Mitchell went through what is now Spring Mill State park with the big and beautiful trees. She talks about the time they all went except her. For some reason she was not able to walk the distance and the team was not able to go. I know the farmers did not use the team for travel if it was in farm working season. The energy of the horses was saved for farm work.

In 1882 when she was fifteen years old she wrote the story called Good Society. It is a two page hand written message. I wonder if it could be a school assignment. I do not know her schooling.

She talks about cleaning and papering the house inside and out and how much better the house looked. She talks about Pa and the little boys doing the nightly chores. Ma had gone visiting with Mrs. Hall. Ella, her younger sister had gone to the mulberry tree.

The Chess family lived not far from the home of George Donaldson, the Scotchman and world traveler. He lived in the dense forest above the cave that has been named Donaldson Cave which is now Spring Mill State Park. He loved nature and wanted the forest to remain always as it was in his time. The Chess family supplied him with the food from the farm. The children delivered him milk, butter, eggs, maple syrup and other supplies.

Maggie had written:
"To weave, to spin, to knit and sew, was once the girl's employment but now to flirt and catch a boy is all she calls enjoyment".

She had a boyfriend, Webster Washington Baker, who left her at the age of 18 to travel with his family to Kansas and homestead some land. We have the poem written by him about the girl he left behind. He came back to Indiana sometime between 1888 and 1890. They became sweethearts again and were married on Feb. 7, 1892. He would have been thirty and she would have been twenty-five years old.

Chapter 3 —
Good Society

Good Society by Maggie Chess 1882 (fifteen years old)

IT IS HARD TO estimate the value of good society we do not mean the society of the rich, but we mean moral society. We mean the society of the good, the upright, the pure in heart. When we speak of a lady in the true sense of the word we do not simply mean a person that wears fine dress or costly jewels; but we mean a person of true lady like qualities and when we speak of a gentleman we do not simply mean a man of wealth, a man that wears fine clothes or drives a costly team; but we mean a man of good ?????? character , a man whose every day life will bare inspection a man who will shun the grog shop, the gambling house and all such dens iniquity. It is folly for a person to think they can associate with the wicked and be ????????by their evil influence. There is a familiar t??? of scripture which says evil communications corrupt good manures. This. requires no comment and I will not attempt to offer any but will simply remark that a good society is the foundation of good government.

But will simply remark that a good way to judge a person is by the company they keep. It is better to be alone than in the company of the wicked.

Chapter 4 —
My Trip To The Moon

By Maggie Chess

LONG SINCE MY IMAGINATION has been some what excited concerning the moon. I have heard many things said about it. About its inhabitans its borrowing light from the Sun just to give it to the earth and it is also said that old maids will stand and gaze at it for hours and if you ask them why they do so; the reply is why there is a man up there. So I resolved to visit that object that looks so much like a big cheese. But the thought how to go puzzled me for a few minutes but I soon decided to go by telegraft, I had but little to say about what passed up there only that I went with such a whizzing and buzzing as I never heard before almost instantly I was headed off at rather a strange looking station the operatoer there was frighteneded at such a dispatch his eyes bugged out so for I believe I could have knocked them off with a stick but he soon got all right again the first thing he said to me was where are you from? I told him I was from the land of Cleveland he seemed to understand for he was a wise man. By this time I was getting very hungry .so I asked him where I could get a good meal. he showed me a house where I could be waited upon; so I called at the door but OH! what a looking object presented itself to me: her feathers ?ong way of the ??????; her nose resembled that of an elephant except it was to red, her ears ??? great cabbage leaves she asked me what I would ?????????????????????????????????????? ???my dinner if you please. She conducted me to the dining room and seated me at the table where many kinds of meats were served wood picks, humming birds, martins and other birds, they leave cold countries for winter protections.

Dinner was soon over. I now made aquantince with other ?????? of the house, they corsponded with the descriptpion of the ????????????????? ??????????????????????????

Featured bit They were kind and courtoius; they treated me with great respect. I romed over the land for several weeks gathering fine specimens mining was the chief ocupation of the people. They manufactured quite ?????? of brass infact most all of some of the animals expecialy the mokeys have brass heads, and considerable brass could also be seen in the faces of some of the people. But about this time I discovered that I was on the obosiit ?of the globe from the telegraft office, and I was to return home so I was buzzed to the end of my ? to know how to come but A wise tought happened to come to me that the moon had to go down about every 24 hours so I just took a seat on the corner of the moon and took my flight downward with such rapidity not to be excelled even by the dawning wing of the American Eagle.

Chapter 5 —
Maggie's Journal

May the 16, 1886
Sunday evening

I HAVE OFTEN THOUGHT how nice a journal would be and always failed to commence one, but now I have made my mind up that I will start. [Where there is a will there is a way]. There are eight of us in family, six children, four boys and two girls. I am the oldest one [age 18].We live in a good farm house in the country four miles from town. Well it is Sunday evening and I am as lonesome as can be. The reason why is because I was not able to walk to Church this morning [it being four miles] and our team was not cable of performing the journey so I had to remain at home this is the first time I have missed for so long it seems odd. The way we do is we all go to Church in the morning and stay for Sunday School in the evening. [We take our dinner most of the time]. The church house is in the east end of Mitchell. It is now five O'clock. Good by journal, some other time. Maggie Chess

Now to my journal again. June the 8, 1886
Well it is Thursday eve. There has nothing much important occurred since my last writing only we have got our house cleaned we have painted it in side and out and papered the hall and the setting room and I tell you it looks a great deal better. I am sitting in the front door. Pa and the little boys are doing up the night work, Ma has gone up to Joe Burton's with misses Hall, Howard has gone to Mitchell to the commencement at the normal Collage and Ella has gone to the mulberry tree. "After Supper"

Chapter 6 —
Chewing and spitting

1-2-3-4- ???????

5. Sometimes within there neighbor's door,
   Things there will tell of pleasures o'er,
   And spit upon the hearth or floor
   Until it spreads a foot or more,
   And still they are liking union.

6. When they are sad they will chew much
   Than they have ever done before,
   And yet their troubles are no?????
   Tobacco makes their tongues ?????
   They can not sing good union.

7. Ofts the curds so large with?????
   The juice runs out and????
   And there we see the filthy ????
   The mouth to full to????
   And sing a pretty union.

8. At the church we some?????
   The slobbers run a ??????
   ? person there will ????
   ?? to make a buz????
   ???sing the heavy????

9. Some ladies dip tobacco snuff,
   While others have a pipe and puff,
   And all others chew the nasty stuff,
   And all their mouths look bad enough,
   To sing a filthy union.

10. If people had the money lent,
    That for tobacco they have spent,
    So many need not to have to rent,
    But live at home with much content,
    And dwell in peace and union.

11. They that could pay their preachers well,
    And hear the truths that he might tell,
    To sinners on their way to hell,
    ???????? there with God to dwell,
    And live with Christ in union.

12. The preacher too, might quit the weed,
    From such expense be always freed,
    And much less money he would then need,
    And nicer things could lead,
    And talk to us of union.

13. We'd not then see him in the stand,
    There acting like a filthy man,
    Who spits upon the desk as grand
    As though he owned all Canaan'a land.
    Before he preaches union.

14. The lady, too, might quit the stuff,
    Lay down her pipe and all her snuff;
    Their path would then not be so rough,
    And still their children have enough
    With out tobacco union.

15. Come one and all and quit the trade,
    And try to be a nicer grade,
    And read your Bible in the shade,
    And then you'll ??? you, are ???? paid
    Than in this costly union.

Maggie Chess
Rivervale, Ind

Part Two:

LIVING ON THE FARM AND THE HAPPENINGS OF LIFE IN LAWRENCEPORT

Chapter 7 —
Chess Farm

"Squeak" "squeak" "Squeak". The young boy, in the early 1900's heard the noise coming from under the ground. Chester knew what it was. It was his lost pig. It had been missing for a couple of weeks or more. The noise was coming from the sink hole. The boy ran through the sugar maple grove to the house to tell his dad, Webster Baker, about the find.

His dad found a rope and together they hurried back to the sink hole. Chester, fastened to the rope, let himself down into the hole. He was in a large room and he soon found the little pig. The pig hadn't eaten for a long time and all the fat was gone from his bones. Chester picked him up and returned to the surface. The little fellow joined the rest of the pigs for a good dinner. He lived to be fat and go off to the market.

This farm was an extension of the karsts region around the grist mill at Spring Mill. It had many sink holes and springs. The beautiful rocks that extended above the ground would some day be a quarry. The rock ledge overhanging Mill Creek had a beauty of its own. An amazing spring gushed out of the hillside to fall into Mill Creek as the small stream meandered its way to White River.

There is a large flat rock in the ground. When a person walks over the rock, they can hear the echo of their footsteps. What is beneath that rock? It has to be an open space for the sound to echo. How many caves are there still to be discovered?

There is a hole in the rock, about a foot and a half square. The hole looks like it goes straight down. However, one can see rocks not far below the surface. It looks like many holes in this area. But it has one distinction. In the dry season, when all other springs have dried up, this one becomes a gushing water spring. It has been a life saver for the farmer.

When Chester Baker was a young boy, he was playing with his wagon on the hill above the opening. The wagon overturned and he lost his shoe. The shoe rolled down the bank and went splash right into the spring. The shoe sank and was to be seen no more. That was a big calamity in the early nineteen hundreds. There was very little money to buy extra shoes.

Chapter 8 —
Huckster

MY FATHER WAS A Huckster in his early years. As a farm boy, he seems to have the desire to do other things.

He had a car in 1917, the year he got out of High School. What kind of a car, maybe a model T Ford. He would load his car with all kinds of farm produce and a few things he could buy, such as cotton stockings. Then he would go to the different farmhouses and sell his wares. I have his books where he kept his records. He would buy two pairs of stockings and sell them before he had enough money to buy two more pairs and do the same thing over again.

This was the beginning of an aspiring businessman.

Chapter 9 —
Sugar Camp

THE SAP IN SUGAR Maple trees starts running late in the winter. It is a cold time to work in the outdoors. A tent was set up behind the washhouse and near some very big rocks. The land was full of huge boulders. This is a land of Limestone in southern Indiana. A quarry and stone crusher were later started near this site, the stone to be used in forming the roads for Spring Mill State Park.

A large rectangle iron stove with a flat top was placed in the tent. The top of the stove would hold the large flat pans that held the sugar water. I remember the pans as being at least two by five feet. They were placed side by side. This means the stove must have been four foot across or more. The sap was kept simmering until it became the wonderful golden Maple syrup we all loved. A fire had to be kept at an even temperature to make the syrup just right.

Grandmother always added an egg to the simmering magical liquid so the syrup would be clear and beautiful. The golden creation would be so clear that a newspaper could be read through the glass bottle that held the final rendition. The family was proud of the clear golden product. I know the Maple Syrup was sold over a great distance of Southern Indiana.

I remember being bundled up in warm clothes so I could go with Granddad as he made the rounds to gather sap. I would ride on the skid. It was a large wooden sled on runners that was pulled by a horse. Granddad would walk beside the skid, maneuvering the horse from tree to tree. It was a rough ride over the rocks, uneven dirt and tree roots. But what fun to be riding that sled that was pulled by the horse, and enjoying a special time with my granddad. I do not remember the cold. I only remember how much fun it was. A "V" was cut into the trunk of each tree and a hollow wooden funnel directed the sugar water to the bucket that was hung on the tree and placed under the cut. The liquid from the bucket was emptied into a larger container on the skid. From tree to tree we went until the larger container was full and then back to the sugar camp we would go.

This was a family project. Aunts, Uncles, cousins were kept busy as long as the sap was running. It was a twenty-four hour job and could last several weeks.

The washhouse was a haven for the weary workers. It was a place where the workers could come in and rest before it was their turn to tend the fire or make the rounds of the trees to collect the sap. The boards were bleached white from the many scrubbings that went along with washday.

Lye soap was also made in this wash house. The soap was made from the wood ashes. Ashes were put in a container and water was poured over them and allowed to drip through the thick wood powder. This became the liquid lye that was used in the soap. Grease was combined with the lye and this became the strong smelling soap that was used to wash the clothes. I do not know what else was done to make the soap. I can only remember the smell of the washhouse and the looks of the light brown bars of soap. It smelled antiseptic clean.

There was something else special inside the washhouse. It was a washing machine. Now this was the time before electricity and a washing machine was something special. It consisted of a beautiful wooden tub, rounded at the bottom and sitting on legs. Hot water from the pot hanging in the fireplace was poured into the tub with the lye soap. There was a wooden basket hanging inside the tub. The basket was fastened on the sides by a rod that ran to the wooden handle on the outside of the larger tub. Clothes were put in the basket and someone moved the handle back and forth and back and forth. The clothes basket would rock through the warm sudsy water. When the arm of the operator got tired, the clothes were wrung through the wringer into a rinse tub and the clothes were cleaned of all soap and then either hung on the out side clothes line in good weather or hung on lines inside the washhouse when the weather was bad.

Best of all, Grandmother, in her high top button shoes and her dress made from printed feed sacks, would make maple sugar candy. I can still taste the treat. Often I have seen maple sugar candy on sale and I would buy some, hoping it would have the taste of my grandmother Maggie's, wonderful candy. Never did it live up to my memories. But the memories of the taste of that special candy cannot be erased. It holds a special place in my memories forever.

Chapter 10 —
Chester and Louisa

WEBSTER BAKER AND MAGGIE Chess were married in 1892. Their only child, Chester Hobart Baker was born September 2, 1898. He was born in Stonington, Indiana in Lawrence County. At an early age the family moved to the Chess farm near Spring Mill. Maggie's mother, Julie Andrews, had died and Webster and Maggie went back to the home place. Chester's childhood was spent on this farm with the many caves and sink holes. It was a beautiful place with Mill Creek running beside it as it meandered its way to White River. The stone cliffs overlooking the creek were beautiful with the huge sugar maple trees everywhere. There was an apple orchard on the hill and the horse barn near the fenced- in orchard. The cow barn was a short ways down the hill from the horse barn. It had a red silo made from redwood trees. How did the redwood from California get all the way to Indiana to make the silo? I understand it was used wood. I wonder what it had been used for before it was made into a silo.

The chicken house was the closest building to the main house. The garden was beside it. Maggie raised chickens to sell, and would have several hundred chickens at a time. The brooder house was close so the baby chick could be transferred to the bigger chicken house. There were many split rail fences separating the corn and the alfalfa fields.

One hillside close to the house had many limestone boulders coming from the ground. This was later to become a stone quarry. The crushed stone was used to make the roads in what is now Spring Mill State Park. The Sugar Maple trees were the source of sugar water and a sugar camp became a family business. Sheep were raised on this farm and the spinning wheel that was on the second floor of the farm house was kept busy. The back yard had a cistern and a well. The cellar that was half underground and the wash house with the huge fireplace were joined by a roof and a walk way. Many things were stored in the walk way. This is where the large bins of oats for the chickens were kept and also the wood for the fireplace. The back yard was closed in on four sides. The house was on the south side of the yard, the stone boulders and the chicken house on the west. The garden in the northwest corner and the fence separating the yard from the farm animals was on the north side. The wash house and cellar were on the east side. The back yard had two cement walk ways, cistern, water well, and a clothes line. This was young Chester's play yard. When he was very young and Maggie had to leave the house for a short time, Chester's dress was put under the leg of the bed so he couldn't crawl and get into trouble.

As Chester grew older he had a tricycle and a wagon. .

The young boy was taught to do his share of work around the farm as well as how to use a gun and hunt. Sink holes were plentiful in this karst region and farm animals had to be protected from getting trapped in one of the openings. Brush and cut tree limbs were piled over the openings in hopes the animals would not fall in.

Life on the farm was full of surprises. There was a time when they were breaking in a new horse to pull the buggy. The new horse was to become part of a two horse team. One horse was a very reliable animal and would obey. The new horse had a mind of his own and did not respond to commands. When the buggy came to a fork in the road, the faithful horse did what it was supposed to do, but the young horse wanted to go the other way. As a result, the uncontrolled team went scampering into an area that had an out house. What became of the out house? The out of control team with the buggy knocked over the out house. I hope there was no one in it.

He continues in his school work until it was time to go to High School in Mitchell. This school was four miles from where he lived. In early high school years he rode a horse and there were sheds where the horses of the students could be stabled for the day. He had a girl friend that lived out on the Bedford road. He would take his horse and buggy to visit her. Sometimes it would be late when he started the five miles back to his home near Spring Mill. He would be tired from the long day at school and the late visit to his girl friend, Louisa Colglazier. Hearing the clip clopping of the horse's hoofs would lull him to sleep. That was no problem, the horse knew the way home. So Chester would snooze and let the horse do the leading. However, there was a time when he was rudely awakened by the roar of a railroad engine crossing in front of him. But the horse was well trained and had stopped in the road to let the railroad engine go on past.

Before he graduated the Motel T Ford became the transportation. In his High School yearbook of 1917 it states," Chester is one of the few country boys who has stuck with us all through high school. He is very fond of fording out the Bedford Road." After all that is where his girl friend, Louisa, lived.

He became a huckster at an early age and began selling his wares from the Model T. He would go from farm house to farm house selling pots and pans and clothing. I think cotton stockings were sold for about ten cents. He would buy them for eight cents. When he sold a pair he would buy two more and sell them. This was the beginning of his life business as a merchant.

Chapter 11 —
Skeleton

WE LIVED FOR A short time in a house we rented from Dr. Andrews. It had an attic and the entry was behind a closed door. As a child of about three, I always hurried past that door because I was afraid there was a skeleton in that mysterious place.

As years went by, I dismissed it as a childish fear. Years later, I told my mother about my feelings. Then she told me there was a skeleton in that attic. After all, it was rented from a doctor. It was his teaching tool, a real skeleton. This is the house where my brother, Chester Junior Baker, was born.

Chapter 12 —
Lawrenceport

When Dad was a little boy, he lived about a mile away at what is now Spring Mill State Park. How did this little boy get to school in Lawrenceport? I would imagine the first time he would have been taken in a horse and buggy in 1904. Later he would walk. If the weather was bad he would cross the road from the school to the Chamberlain house and stay. They had a little boy about the same age as my dad. This boy would later become the father of Richard Chamberlain, the movie star. The Chamberlain father worked on the railroad.

Now, in 1924, Dad bought this property. It was a small house with a wooden walk way that led to a wash house. In the middle of the walk way was the cistern in which water was drawn for the wash tubs.

Dad had a garage across the road in which he worked on cars. What were the cars in the year of 1924? I am sure a lot were Model T Fords.

In 1925 Bedford Times newspaper held a contest. Mother, Louisa Baker, joined and she worked hard getting subscriptions for the paper. She would go every evening to ask the farmers if they would take the Bedford Paper. One evening, Dad, Mother and my baby brother were in the front seat and I was in the back seat, the car hit a mule that was in the road. I guess the mule was not hurt very much. He just wandered off. But our windshield was shattered. The glass went all over my dad and mother and baby brother. None of us were hurt.

Mother did win that contest. The prize was a new Studebaker car and it had windows that rolled up and down. Wonders were happening all the time. Now we could drive to Mitchell and past Lehigh cement plant and not have dust get into our eyes.

This was a time that a wonderful thing came into our lives, Electricity. Dad wired this little house for this new marvel. Each room had one electric wire hanging from the ceiling. At the end was a round glass ball with a pull chain. When the chain was pulled the room lit up like magic. How wonderful.

Dad was a farm boy, but he always worked in a different way. Now he was working on cars. He also had a huge wooden chest that would hold five hundred pounds of ice. He would drive to the ice house in Orleans and get five hundred pounds of ice in one hundred pound chunks and bring them home and fill the chest. The chest was in the yard next to a tree and the lid was raised by a pulley attached to the tree. People would come and chip off the amount of ice they wanted and take it home to put in their ice boxes. I remember, as a little girl riding in the back of the truck, going through what is now Spring Mill Park and looking up at the wonderful canopy of tree limbs. It was beautiful. The strong smell of ammonia in the ice house is also in my memories.

With the coming of electricity, my mother had an ice cream parlor in a lean-to next to the garage. This was only about a half mile from Bishop Roberts Methodist Church Camp. When the young people were finished with the evening vespers they would walk up the road to Lawrenceport and the ice cream place. There would be a steady stream of young people coming to get an ice cream cone and then going back to the camp for the night.

This house had a fenced area in the back for our two cows, Cherry and Rose. There was a time when one of the cows was missing, Mother and I started to walk the hill side that bordered the creek. We found the missing cow and her new born calf in a thicket. This was another miracle that God had given us.

Chapter 13 —
Walk In The Woods

IN 1923 MOST PEOPLE walked where ever they were going. The trip to my Great Aunt Ella's house was through virgin timber. I skipped beside my mother as we made our way through the big and tall handsome trees. Only a little sunlight filtered through the leaves to reach the ground. But on the side of a huge tree was something long and shinning. It was a big snake sunning itself in the shaft of light. Mother stopped and of course I, being only three years old, stopped also. Mother picked up a stick and gave one wallop to that snake's head. It curled over and she continued beating it. I stood back in wonder. The snake had recently had a good meal. The sides were rounded out where it had not yet digested the small animal it had swallowed. Mother was in a furious state. She continued beating until she beat the thing into two parts. That snake was not going anywhere again.

We continued our walk to Great Aunt Ella's house in Lawrenceport. Mother was known to be a very calm but determined woman. She was only five feet tall, but she could meet any emergency.

Chapter 14 —
How I Knew Where Babies Come From?

I WAS A LITTLE girl of 'not quite four' and lived in Lawrenceport, Ind. This was a big town of not even forty houses. But in the early 1800's, that was a big town. The one road was the only one from Louisville to Lafayette. To get across White river, a ferry had to be used. The town did have cross roads that led to the river where there was a Sawmill. The main road led to another part of the river and the flat ground at this location had been a stockyard. People would bring their cattle and put them on a flat boat to be transported down the White, Wabash, Ohio River on to the Mississippi River and sold at New Orleans. The Baltimore and Ohio Railroad came through just north of the town and south of the bend in the river. The railroad station was called Rivervale. In later years of 1800, a Methodist Church Camp was started by Bishop Roberts, between the railroad and Lawrenceport.

We lived on the main road. My mother was about to give birth to my little brother. It was a wet and cold night on January 30, 1924. I wanted to crawl up onto my mother's lap, but there wasn't room. My Dad had gone to get Doctor Colglazier, who lived in Lipsic, Indiana. The roads were bad. People came in to help my mother. Now, what do you do with an 'almost four year old' little girl at a time like this? They put me in the baby bed in the corner of the room. Of course I stood up and watched everything that was going on. People didn't have time to pay any attention to me.

I remember standing up and watching. I do not remember what I saw, but I have been told that I knew all about it the next day and told everyone all about how my little brother came into this world. I guess all of Lawrenceport knew what I knew. I do not remember what I saw, but I always knew where babies came from. I was very proud of my little brother.

Chapter 15 —
Gold Mine

I WAS ONLY FIVE years old, but I found a gold mine. Well, maybe not a gold mine. But I did find a half dollar. That is almost a gold mine. I was walking down a little path about three or four doors from where I lived in Lawrenceport. It was a dirt path I remember the ground being very soft and dusty. It must have been in the dry season of summer. I was probably barefooted. Most of us went barefooted in the summer time. It was a way of saving money for shoes. It was really just a way of life at that time in 1925.

There was something shiny laying there in the dust. It was a half dollar. My, it looked big. I picked it up and ran home to tell my mother. A half dollar was a lot of money. Why would I at Ninety years old remember that half dollar? A coin of that magnitude was an enormous amount of money for a little five year old gal. It is still in my memories as something very special.

Chapter 16 —
Dolly

NELLIE, "MOTHER, MY DOLL is outside in the rain. I'm going to get it"

Mother, "No, it is raining too hard, you will get soaked"

Nellie, whining, "I want my doll"

Mother, very sternly. "You cannot go get it. You shouldn't have left it out there.

I knew Mother was right, but this four year old girl wanted her dolly. The rain was coming down so hard I could barely see the spot in the yard where my doll lay. But here comes a form walking across the yard. It might be raining hard, but I knew that form was Rose, one of our cows. Rose was a gentle cow and most of the time I loved her, but now? No, she was headed for my doll. "No Rose, No" I screamed as her big rough tongue came across the doll's face. The paint on the face of that doll must have tasted good. She keep licking and licking. I was crying and at that moment I didn't love her any more. I hated her. She was eating my doll.

The rain did not last forever, and I did get to go out and retrieve what was left of my doll. The doll was wet but intact. However, the face was gone. That no good cow had licked the face off my doll. I wonder what kind of paint was used to make the face. It must have tasted good. I was devastated, I had the wet doll, but it has no face. Crying did not help.

It was a lesson that was hard to learn. I still left toys where they shouldn't be. But, maybe not as forgetful as I was before that mean old cow licked the face off my dolly.

Chapter 17 —
Two Room School House

My first year of school in 1925 was exciting. I lived in Lawrenceport, Indiana and all I had to do was walk across the road and down two houses and I was at the school. I was five years old and was finding things very exciting. My first grade teacher's name was Lois Reynolds. I thought she was the prettiest thing I had ever seen.

The first six grades were in one room and seventh and eighth grades were in another room. Harley Allen was the teacher of the older kids. I think there were about ten kids in my first grade or at least there were two rows of desks for first graders. The seats got larger as they progresses down the room for the older kids.

There was a wood heating stove in our corner of the room. The boys would bring in the wood for the stove.

As the teacher progressed from first grade to sixth grade, we could listen to the lessons of the older students. But sometimes we could take our paper and pencil to the window and hold our paper over a picture and trace it onto our paper. Oh, what fun, I am sure this was the start of my art work.

The out houses were outside and we had to hold up our hand if we had to excuse ourselves. There was a time, I had to go, but the teacher did not see my hand or thought it was unnecessary. She didn't give me permission so I had to wait. Wait, I could not. Oh, how embarrassing to see that puddle of water increasing under my desk. One boy made fun of me. How cruel some children can be!

Recess was a fun time. One of the games was "Handy Over". The school building must not have been very big if we could throw a ball over the school and then run around on the other side of the building. I do not remember what the object of the game was. All I remember, someone threw the ball over the school building and we would run to the other side. We had fun anyway.

Oh, how I would love to have my first grade reader back. Those stories were very special to me. The Sky was Falling, The Troll Under the Bridge, The Little Brown Hen, Chicken Little and The Three Little Pigs were only a few of the wonderful stories opened up to me.

Part Three:

MITCHELL

Chapter 18 —
My Grandparents, Jacob and Nellie Colglazier

My Grandmother was a very quiet, unassuming, but strong person in my life. This beautiful person had long, thick red hair. At family gatherings, her two granddaughters were kept quiet by allowing us to comb and arranging it in any fashion we would like. Wilma, my cousin, would take one side and I would comb the other. The thickness and heaviness of the hair would cause a problem in my Grandmother's later life. She would develop headaches. Finally the doctors decided the heavy hair was causing it. The back part was cut out and still there was plenty of hair to do up in the fashion of the 1920s.The headaches stopped.

Her seven grand children did not seem to bother her and we spent hours and days at the farm roaming the hills, climbing the trees, picking blackberries, riding the work horses and climbing all over the barn. The three oldest of these grandchildren were within one year of each other. They included the two granddaughters in which I was one of them. The other four were boys. Three of those boys were within four months of being the same age and the fourth boy was only two years younger. They certainly had a good time teasing their granddad. He was special, too. He would play the piano and sing little ditties for the grandchildren. He was a short man with stubby hands, but his hands could cover the keyboard. I don't ever remember his fingers moving but the music would come out of that old piano and he would sing his little songs. He was a farmer and an auctioneer. I loved to go and hear him cry a sale. He would point his cane at the bidders and get talking so fast that he would spit all over himself. That cane is one of my cherished possessions to this day. .

There was always fresh baked bread with plenty of homemade butter and jellies in the icebox on the porch. Grandmother had to have the patience of Job. I never remember her raising her voice at any of us. That didn't mean she never corrected us. There was a time when the two girls found some make up in a chest upstairs and we had to try it out. I am sure we came downstairs all painted up. She didn't think that was very ladylike. Neither did she think it ladylike to sit on the bank in front of the house and wave at all the cars that passed by on the Dixie Highway. She did have her ideas of how things should be.

She was very proud that she graduated from Common School. Back in the early days of this country that was special. At that time she was allowed to take the test for her teacher's license and passed it. She was a very intelligent and understanding person.

I learned the names of many old flowers, such as 'snow on the mountain', passion vine with its intriguing pedals, how to prune grapes, cut up chicken, be sure and wait until the old rooster was at the other side of the chicken yard, before going to the 'out house'. I inspected the smoke house to see how the fire was built in the concrete pit in the center of the floor, I learned the difference between salt pork and pickled pork. I cut up cabbage for sour kraut. The gentleness of this lady and gentleman remains a beautiful memory in my thoughts. I wish all children could have the tutoring us grandchildren had.

Chapter 19 —
Big Old Barn

THE BIG OLD BARN stood majestically on the top of the hill for over a hundred years. The faded red paint was nearly gone from its wooden sides. But it was still a proud barn and if it could talk it would have many stories to tell. Not only about the animals it sheltered, but the children that make it into a play house.

It was a huge barn and even in its prime, it was know as the Big Red Barn on the hill. The center beam, high in the rafters was big enough for grandchildren to walk across it from one end to the other. Now, that had to come from a big, big tree.

There were four big sections to this barn, one for pigs, one for horses, one for cows and one for machinery. There were also two roadways for wagons to go through. Yes, it was a big barn.

The south section was for pigs. There were several pig pens and a walkway that ran the width of the barn. I remember going with my grandmother as she carried the skim milk from the milk separator to give it to the pigs. At that time skim milk was only good for the pigs. Now, that is the only kind I buy and I pay a premium price for it.

The next section north was for horses. Several horses could be kept in here away from the cold and storms of winter. The grandchildren loved those horses and if it was not working season, we were allowed to ride them and play with them.

Next was the space left for the wagons with their loads of hay. Even this was enclosed by big barn doors. The hay was pitched from the wagon onto the upper floors of the barn. It takes a lot of hay to feed cattle for the winter. The seven grandchildren loved to play in the barn. Of course the barn was full of snakes. We learned a lot from our wise old Grandmother, Nellie Colglazier. She told us to leave those snakes alone, they are our friends. They kept the mice and rats from eating the grain and that kept fires from starting in the old barn. Of course, no self respecting snake would dare show itself with those wild and noisy grandchildren.

I remember how much fun it was to jump from the big rafter beam into a pile of hay on the ground. That was a long jump, but this girl child thought it was fun. It was fun, until the day I jumped and there was a pitch fork beside me as I landed. I never jumped after that.

The next section was for cows, with the big manger running the width of the barn. The cows would put their heads through the stanchions and chew on the hay in the manger. They would be quiet while even a little girl like me could learn how to milk them.

I learned how to milk when I was about eight years old. My mother and dad had two cows, one was named Rose and the other one, Cherry. Rose was the easy one to milk so that was the one I would milk, while my mother would milk Cherry. These cows were kept at the farm with the rest of my grandparents cows. I was proud that I knew how to milk. I could even squirt milk into the barn cat's mouth. But I did not like the tail of that cow. That tail was made up of string like ropes and when that cow tried to flick the flies off its back it would come across my face. Often it had been dipped in manure. Yuck! It hurt and it smelled. I learned how to hold the tail and try to milk with one hand. I also had to keep my balance on the three legged stool and keep the cow from kicking over the bucket of milk. It was not easy. I was never able to strip the cow. Mother always had to finish up for me and get the last bit of milk out of the udder. I am proud to this day that I was taught how to milk when I was a little girl.

The next section of the barn was left open, but it was a place to run the empty wagons and machinery in for the winter.

On top of this structure was a cupola and on top of that was the weather vane. Many, many doves and pigeons would make their home in this space and their mournful cooing would echo through the big old barn.

Yes, it was a big old barn. It is no more, having burnt to the ground a number of years ago. But it will always remain in my memory as I am sure it will be in the memories of the rest of the grandchildren.

Chapter 20 —
Fun On The Farm

OUR GRANDPARENT'S FARM WAS a fun place to play. Seven grand children could roam all the wonderful places a farm can contain, the barn, the back woods and many places in between. The ravine that held so many Indian arrowheads was a place to spend many hours. There was the pond that my brother, Chester J. (Bake) Baker, would be so proud that he could dive in and swim across without coming up for air. Later years he learned he could also jump across the whole thing. How wonderful are the childhood memories.

Granddad would let us ride the workhorses if it were not working season for the horses. Boy cousins, about the same age of eight years old would get on the back of the horse and ride it to the woods for a day of fun. The older kids had to walk.

This was the time of "make your own toys". Rubber guns were the thing we could all make. We carved from a piece of wood something that looked like a gun, cut a round from an old inner tube to make the ammunition, take half a clothespin for the trigger and fasten it to the gun with a strong rubber band. Then a round piece of wood would be placed between the two so the trigger would rock. The piece of the inner tube would be stretched from the front of the 'gun' to the trigger where it was placed between the back of the gun and the trigger mechanism. When the trigger was pushed the gun would release the inner tube bullet and away it would go. It was very effective and, boy, did it hurt if a person got hit. After so many hits, I quit playing with rubber guns.

The horse didn't like it, either. With four boys on its back and the gun accidentally discharging in the neighborhood of its rump, the horse took off from the woods to the barn. That horse could have won the Kentucky Derby and the boys were trying to stay on. The boys came off one at a time on the way back to the barn. My brother was the only one that stayed on. The horse came to a sudden stop at a gate and then he sailed off. It was a good thing the horse did not get to the barn and rake

'Bake' off as it went through the barn door. But there was one problem. 'Bake' lost his shoes on that wild ride.

One pair of shoes a year was all a person could afford. This was a calamity. All the grandchildren were told to follow the path back to the woods and FIND that shoe. We did not even try to find any arrowheads as we followed the path of that racing horse. WE DID FIND THE SHOES.

THE HORSE DID LET US RIDE HIM AGAIN.

Chapter 21 —
The Way It Was

A SIX YEAR OLD girl in 1926 found a lot of ways to amuse herself. We lived in Mitchell, Indiana and it was the time before there was city water or at least in our area on West Main Street. Run off water from the roof was saved in a barrel and then used for washing clothes. The water was taken from the barrel and put in an iron pot and heated over a fire outside. Then it was transferred into the washing machine which was electric. Electricity had come to the town a few years before. The washing machine had a basket that swished back and forth in the warm sudsy water, a wonderful invention.

The six year old girl found a lot of things to help her pass the time. One was to play in that barrel of water. It was fun to watch the wiggly worms as they wiggled their way up and down in the water. A stick moving in the water would make the little worms wiggle even more. They would go up and down in the water, oh, what fun to watch them wiggle.

A few years later when I told that story, I found out those wiggly things were mosquito larva. I didn't know that. Now, I would know to get rid of those pests. They would later turn into mosquitoes and they would bite me. But this was the time of innocents. I was enjoying each new thing that I discovered.

Chapter 22 —
Wash Your Ears

"Nellie Margaret, wash your ears". That was my mother's voice.
A person would think I had been playing in the mud. Well, maybe.
I did like the outdoors. I was only seven and I was still discovering
the wonders of the earth. I loved it, even the mud and dirt. I was an
obedient little girl, I think. So, I took the wash cloth and rolled a corner
up and started to wash my ears. I stuck the cloth in the hole in my head
and twisted it around and washed my ears. I was proud of myself. Back
to mother I went. She took one look and said, "Nellie Margaret, I said
go wash your ears".

I answered under my breath, " I did wash them".

"Well, go wash them again".

Back to the wash pan I went and rolled up the wash cloth and stuck
it into the holes in my head again. I gave it an extra twist and back to my
mother I went. This time I was in trouble. She took the wash cloth and
proceeded to wash all of my ears, even the shell that surrounds that hole
in my head. She even washed behind that shell. I didn't know that was
part of my ears. She wasn't very easy with her washing. **But I learned
that all of the skin at the side my face is my ears and to wash them
meant all of it. I have since learned that that shell is like a finger
print. No two are alike, some of them are soft and can bend easy,
some of them are hard and do not bend. Mine are the hard kind
and to bend them hurts. That was a hurting lesson.**

41

Chapter 23 —
Two room house

My job was to go behind the outhouse and get the pot before we turned in for the night. I would have liked to bring it into the house before dark, but that was a 'No No'. We lived next to the Mitchell Cemetery and I knew spooks were watching me. I would hurry and grab Mary Jane, that was the name my mother called the white porcelain pot. Then I would run into the house and slam the door.

The next night would be the same.

We lived one half of a block from C& B Auto Company. Dad had built a little two room house in 1927. It was on the section that had been the Mitchell Fair grounds. We had a living room and a kitchen. There was a screened porch all across the back of the house. The porch divided into two parts. Most of it was our bedroom and the smaller was the back porch which contained our washing machine.

The house was next to the Mitchell Cemetery. My parents, my brother and I slept on that screened in sleeping porch winter and summer. Junior (called Bake), was four years younger than I. Mother had made pongee curtains fastened at the top and bottom by rods. The curtains could be pushed open or closed. I never remember being cold. My cot had a feather bed and I would sink in its insulation with blankets on top of me. There was an oil cloth over the top of the bed to keep out any rain or snow that came in between the curtains. But I do remember how cold the rim of that chamber pot was if I had to get up during the night. Of course we did not have a bathroom, only the little house out in back with the moon shaped window. There was a wooden walk way to the out house and the garage.

The "Honey Dipper" was a very necessary part of our life. He was a man called Peg Leg because he had only one leg and the other one was nothing by a peg. He would come by with his wagon pulled by horses and clean out the out houses. Where he took the smelly stuff, I have no idea. But the out house was cleaned and did not smell.

We did not have running water when we first moved into that little house. Dad had dug a cistern that caught the water run off from the house. That was our water supply. A year after moving in, city water came out Main Street and we had one water spigot in our yard. My! That water was a marvel. In the summer time the neighbor kids would love to jump in and out of the water spray. We had all the water we wanted for cooking and bathing.

Our bathing was in a wash tub placed behind the stove. To my remembrance all of us used the same water. Then the water was thrown outside. This was a Saturday night ritual.

Monday was wash day. The wash water was heated outside in an old iron pot. The wood for the fire was laid the night before so it would be ready for mother to strike a match to it. She would get up in the middle of the night and light the fire. It would be a big fire and the water would be roaring and boiling in the morning so it could be transported to the washing machine on the back porch. The washing machine was electric and it had a basket that swished back and forth in the warm sudsy water. Of course the clothes were hung outside on a clothes line. In winter the clothes would freeze, but would blow themselves dry. In very severe weather they would then be draped over everything in the house in order to dry.

Dad climbed one of the big old trees that lined the west side of the cemetery. That is where he placed our swing. It was a wonderful swing because the ropes were very long and a child could swing a long ways out.

Of course all the neighborhood children used that swing. There was a cinder road way between our yard and the swing. Cinders were what the driveways were made of in Mitchell. Lehigh was the easy source of cinders. Lehigh Cement was the only big business in Mitchell at that time.

We could only afford one pair of shoes and they were bought in late summer for the school year. We went bare footed most of the time. We did wear shoes for Sunday school. In early spring when it was time to go barefoot, the cinders would cut our feet. But by the end of summer our feet were so callused that we could run up and down in that driveway with comfort.

There was a big signboard across the road. One Fourth of July I threw a fire cracker at that sign and it exploded and part of it came back to me and hit me just below the eye. How fortunate I was just to have a cut on my face and not in the eye. I learned a life long lesson of how dangerous fire crackers can be.

At night time the neighborhood kids would play hide and seek. Many would hide in the cemetery behind the tombstones. But I don't remember anyone going very deep into the graveyard.

During this time Dad drove to Indianapolis once a week to attend a class in learning how to work on Radios. He bought two Majestic radio -victrolas, one for our house and one to sell at the garage. When he sold the one at the garage, he would buy two more. When that sold, he would buy four more. This is the start of his new business in Bedford. He opened an appliance store on the north side of the square in 1930. We left Mitchell and moved to Bedford.

During the time we lived in Mitchell, mother would catch the Bedford bus and go to business school. She learned a lot about running a business and bookkeeping.

I have many wonderful memories of my growing up. This is only a few.

Chapter 24 —
Jack's Story

THERE WERE THREE BOY cousins, Chester "Bake" Baker, Jack Colglazier and Norman Norris. Jack was the oldest, born on Christmas Day, 1923. My brother was next born on January 30, 1924. Norman was the youngest born on May 10, 1924. They were a wild group.

Here is what Jack has to say about their Granddad.

I remember granddad well, I most remember how mad he would get at Bake, Norman and me for absolutely no reason. He had three little angels and tried to turn them into little devils. Ha! If he had spanked me and sent me home every time he threatened, I would still be sore and traveling. Painting his tomatoes yellow seemed to upset him. Goosing the accelerator with his cane while he was driving seemed to upset him. Hiding his glasses, having egg fights, shooting his favorite Bob White, in fact, it seems everything we did upset him. What a wonderful person. It is a shame everyone couldn't have had grandparents to love and look up to like we did. He had a great wit .He would play that piano with his stubby fingers and sing little funny ditties to us grandchildren.

Through out it all Mama, his name for our grandmother, would patiently nod her head and continue knitting, crocheting or whatever she would be doing at the time. I certainly didn't want her mad at me. She had that ability of looking at you and send a better behave message. I have never forgotten the correction we got from her when Bake, Norman and me had a pillow fight in the small upstairs bedroom and scattered feathers everywhere. Great memories.

I remember every nook and cranny of that old barn. We had many corn cob fights in it and jumped from the loft many times.

Granddad let me drive the team of horses to pull the fork full of hay to the loft. It was very important that the horses be turned in the opposite directions with each pull up. This was to keep the rope from tangling. Somehow, very, very often, Granddad would not be watching when I made the turn and then swore I hadn't turned as I was supposed to. This let to an argument with him getting very mad and threatening to paddle my A—and send me home. Of course it never happened. Finally, he would stomp his foot and remark Sh—I'm going to the house and go to bed. Which he did. This happened nearly every time, but he always let me have the same job the next time. It was a part of our every day life and one we looked forward to.

Raking new mown hay into windrows was another source of disagreement. Nearly all of the hay fields were on hilly ground which made it hard to keep the windrows in perfect alignment. There was no problem with dumping the rake while going up the hill but coming down was not so easy. The horses would be moving much faster and timing the fork and dump at exactly the right time was nearly impossible so the rows would angle off. Granddad did not like this and let me know it real quick. The argument would start and end about the same way every time.

I also remember rolling a tire down the bank in front of Mama Colglazier's house in front of a car and almost causing a wreck. That was before the highway was paved. Seems to me the tire actually hooked on or went around the front tire of the car. I do remember Granddad getting pretty mad.

Is there any wonder why I loved Moma and Granddad so much? How they put up with three boys at the same time speaks highly of their tolerance. I wasn't really mean, just mischievous.

What memories I have of this wonderful, loving man, he had to get a kick out of it or he would have never put up with it time after time.

Chapter 25 —
More Memories from Jack Colglazier

THESE MEMORIES OF JACK'S were before he started school in the first grade. He lived on the south side of West Main Street in Mitchell. The house was next to the Four Points Garage.

Aunt Louisa was a scary person to me. I remember when she caught me hammering the sidewalk and chipping stone from the tombstones in the cemetery. She threatened to call the police. I hid in a shed for the rest of the day, thinking the cops were coming after me. Many years later, I learned how nice she could be.

I remember setting fire to the field between the house and the Four Points garage. Knocking out a street light, setting a firecracker off in my hand and goodness knows what else.

I remember shooting granddad's favorite whippoorwill out of the top of the tall pine tree near the house. Granddad was sitting under it. I was standing out by the barn, raised the gun and shot without aiming. I couldn't have hit the bird one time in a hundred if I had been trying. He got mad at me again. Is there any wonder why I loved mama and granddad so much? How they put up with the three of us boys at the same time speaks well of their tolerance, I wasn't really mean, just mischievous.

There were the egg fights with Mama's eggs and the pillow fight upstairs in the small bedroom. We scattered feathers everywhere. But Mama had a way of looking at us and we knew we had better change our way. She was a very special person.

This is a continuation of Jack's stories. He was born in Mitchell, Indiana. This tells how he came to be living in Russellville, Alabama.

In a major way, your mother had a hand in my family being here. I was hired by Indiana Limestone Co. by Mr. Sakel in 1947. At that time he was living in an apartment at your house on Sixteenth Street, so your mother influenced my employment.

Even though I no longer worked at the Limestone Company, Mr. Sakel contacted me in 1954 to ask if I was interested in a job at Alabama Limestone Company. Their estimator, Ed Crean, had suffered a stroke and they had contacted Indiana Limestone Institute to recommend someone for replacement. Naturally, they would not recommend someone presently working for them so Mr. Sakel, thankfully, thought of me.

This connection also saved my job when I came back to Indiana Limestone in 1970. The president, at that time, hired me from Alabama Limestone. Unfortunately, this president was fired two weeks after I came back. The man that fired him was Chairman of the Board, Bert Sakel, who was living in Indianapolis at that time. He not only fired the president but, also, anyone that he had hired.

My job was saved by my past acquaintance with Mt. Sakel. He sent word that my job was safe.

There, you have a short story of your Mother's influence in my life. Things work in mysterious ways, don't they?

Chapter 26 —
Nine Year Old Girls

WILMA AND I WERE cousins. Wilma's house was on the south side of Main Street, next to the C&B Garage. My house was across Main Street next to the Mitchell Cemetery.

There were four siblings in Wilma's family. She had three brothers, James (Tim), Jack and Phil. I had only one brother. My name was Nellie Margaret Baker and my brother was Chester Junior Baker.

My mother had flyers made to advertise Dad's business. He had taken on Majestic Radios to sell as well as the garage business. The next year he was to leave the garage business and move to Bedford to start an electrical business in the Grey Stone Hotel called C& B Electric Co.

But this story takes place the year before he left Four Points. Mother had flyers made to advertise Dad's radio business. She hired the children to deliver them. Mitchell was not a large town and each group of children was given a territory to deliver the flyers. We were to earn fifty cents. That was a lot of money for a young person to earn. Jack said he remembers delivering some, but soon got tired of it and burned the rest of the flyers. He hid in a culvert until he thought it was time to go home. He said my mother found out about it before he got home and didn't pay him.

Wilma and I were given a section on the south side of Mitchell to deliver the advertisements. We did deliver ours. It was a beautiful spring day and we were enjoying ourselves. There was a field on the south side of Mitchell on either Seventh or Eighth Streets that was full of violets. We spent time in that field playing in the flowers. We picked them and made violet chains.

I do not know how much time we spent just playing in the flowers, we were sure enjoying ourselves. But spring weather can change quickly. The temperature was dropping and Wilma and I had left home that morning in short sleeves and no jackets. We were getting cold. Soon we were very cold and we started to hurry home. It was probably a mile back to our homes. Part of the time we were running and then becoming tired we were walking fast. We were on Main Street which was the most traveled street in Mitchell. While we were running toward home, the truck from C & B Auto Co. passed us. Why didn't they stop and pick up these two cold, cold girls? I know they did not see us. But we wanted a ride very much. We were very uncomfortable and ready to cry.

We did make it to our warm houses. I guess we got paid, but the only thing I remember is how cold I was.

Chapter 27 —
C & B Auto Co.

IN THE LATE 1920S my Dad owned a garage with my mother's brother, Clay Colglazier. It was called Four Points. It was at the intersection of West Main St. in Mitchell and St. Road 37. At that time road 37 was the main road between Louisville and Chicago. The big trucks would come in and fill up with gasoline. The station was open all night. I guess you would call it a truck stop. Can you imagine what a truck looked like in 1928? It did not have eighteen wheels as the trucks do today in 2010. They only had four wheels. It was not an easy ride. The gasoline tank was under the seat. The seat had to be taken out and the tank filled up with fuel. Then the seat would be put back in place and the driver could continue with his trip. It was called "Riding the Bomb".

When there was a wreck, dad would be called to bring his wrecker and pull the car out of the ditch. He said the wreck would always end up in poison ivy. He was very allergic to the weed. Mother, who was the bookkeeper of the garage, would often go with him. She was not allergic to poison ivy and could help with the connections between the car and wrecker.

The wrecker was made from an old Cadillac coupe. The crane was put in where the rumble seat once was. The rumble seat was a seat that opened up and was out in the open behind the main cab of the car.

Memories

Chapter 28 —
Christmas to Remember

I WAS EIGHT YEARS old and this year our tree would be a pine tree. Always before, Dad would go to the farm and cut a red cedar tree that lined most of the fence rolls. But this year, we were going to have a real pine tree. It had long sharp needles and was beautiful. We were to have our first electric lights for the tree. It was special. Each bulb was in the form of some animal or bird. There was a turkey, chicken, bird, cow, horse and many more. What a wonderful sight.

School vacation was here and I was excited. The first day I did not feel very good. I had red spots on my skin and they were itching. The next day they were worse and I felt terrible. No, No it couldn't be. But it was. I had the chicken pox. I would look out the window at other kids playing in the snow. I wanted to, but all I could do was scratch. Mother said "don't scratch". But it itched. I did not miss a day of school. When school started in January, I was back to normal.

That year, I got a present in the shape of a baseball and it was wrapped in gold foil. The next year I got another one and the following year another one. This became a tradition for at least twenty more years. Even after I was married I would get a little round present wrapped in gold foil. That gold ball was a turnip which was very special to me. I knew it was from my Great Aunt Ella. After she was gone, her daughter, Alberta kept the ball coming. It seems that when I was much younger and at Aunt Ella's house in Lawrenceport, I would help myself to the raw turnips. They were GOOD. I still like raw turnips. I do not care for them cooked, but RAW, "Yes". This little round ball was a ball of Love. Love can be displayed in many ways. This is one of the many ways my family showed their love for me. I have been blessed many times.

I am going to the store now, and buy me a turnip.

Chapter 29 —
Dreams

DREAMS! WHAT DO LITTLE eight or nine year old girls dream of. I can remember thinking, "If I had a fairy god mother, I would not wish for riches or beauty, I would wish I could sing. In my mind, I could hear beautiful music. But when I opened my mouth that is not what came out. The sound that came out didn't have any soothing melodious qualities at all.

When I was in church and the beautiful songs were being sung, I sure opened my mouth and bellowed out. I don't know whether people looked at me and thought, "I wish she would shut up". I didn't know I couldn't sing, but I did know that what came out of my mouth was not what I heard in my brain.

In later years when I was in Junior High School, and the students in a large group were practice singing , the voice teacher would stop the group and say, "Whoever is singing off key, please stop." Was she talking about me? I didn't know. I did wonder, "Could it be me"?

I had eight years of piano. I learned to read music very well. My cousin didn't learn to read music as well as I did. But there was a reason. She could play by ear. Why learn to read the music, if she could play the music without reading it.

Yes, it finally dawned on me that I could not sing.

But God had other plans to answer my request. He gave me a husband that had a beautiful voice. All of his family had beautiful voices. Even his uncle and aunt had a radio program where they sang gospel music. When we got together they all sang. They are all gone now except one brother, Jack. He has an especially beautiful tenor voice.

God also gave me two sons that have beautiful voices. Their voices did not come from me. Their voices came from God through their Dad. When the three men, my sons and their Uncle Jack start to sing, everyone stops to listen. The harmony is beautiful.

When Randy, my youngest boy, was singing in the church choir with other young children, the choir director came to me and said I should give him voice lessons. We did give him lessons and he had a chance to sing with the Children's Choir in Indianapolis. But we decided not to do that. Those children sing all over the world, but they also give up their childhood to perform with the special group. We are not sorry we made that decision. He has had a much more normal life.

He is now a man of sixty four and music is part of his life. Music cannot be taken away from a person. He sings with the Cedar Rapid Chorale and his church choir. That is a big part of his life.

When he and his brother, Gordon, and their Uncle Jack start to sing, I know God has answered my wish in His own way. I may not be able to sing, but I have this beautiful music I can hear from my family. My dreams are very real.

Part Four:
BEDFORD

Chapter 30 —
Next Door Brat

How LONELY A LITTLE girl of ten can be! My parents had moved all of ten miles from Mitchell to Bedford, Indiana. That is a long ways for a ten year old girl that knew she would never see her friends again.

There were two little eight year old brats living in the neighborhood. The blond brat lived next door to my new home and the other brat, with flying brown hair, lived across the street. These girls would peek around the corner of the house at this lonely girl sitting on the porch and giggle as only an eight year old girl can do. Then they would run and come around the other side of the house and giggle some more. That did not help my loneliness. I was wishing I were back in Mitchell. Later, these girls became my friends and we had many wonderful hours playing, Kick the Can, Tappie on the Ice box , Hide and Seek or just sitting in the swing on the porch.

Our street was Sixteenth St., the same Sixteenth Street that is now a five lane highway. At that time, in 1930, it was only a two-lane brick street with huge trees lining both sides of the road. The trees formed a canopy of beautiful green limbs that shaded the area. There was very little traffic and we played in the street. Bedford is built on many hills. The roads were not level. When we had a rain, we would build a dam across the road to catch the water. No cars would come along to tear down our dam. We knew that Farmer Dusard would come along in the morning with his horses and wagon, bringing his produce to sell. He would tear the dam down in the evening going back to the farm with his wagon empty. But we would have all day to play in the water. Very seldom would a car come along. Now in this time of the twenty first century, a child would not dare to step their foot into the five lane road without the possibility of being hit by a car or a semi-truck. Is that progress?

Chapter 31 —
Toys

WHAT KIND OF TOYS did I have? It was much more fun to climb a tree, ride a bicycle, skate, play cowboy and Indians.

But the Christmas toy I remember most was a jigsaw puzzle of the United States. It must have been made of wood or very heavy cardboard, for I worked it for months and loved it. I was about eight and could put it together upside down and anyway it would go. That is the way I learned my states and where they are in this great country. I liked to have people quiz me as to where the states were. I knew. That has stayed with me to this day. My mother who also knew the capitols of all the States tried to get me to memorize them also. I tried, but my brain did not absorb the capitols as well as the states themselves. I wish every child could have a toy that was as educational and fun as that one was for me. You guessed it. I have bought my grandchildren jigsaw puzzles of the United States.

Chapter 32 —
The Most Stupid Thing I Ever Did

OH WHAT WONDERFUL SUMMERS when a girl is a teenager. I lived only a block from the swimming pool. For two siblings that grew up in a swimming family, life couldn't have been any better. My dad and my mother, both knew how to swim. I know that was unusual for women in the early 1900's.

I do not remember learning how to swim. We were always in the water. Of course the water was White River or a farm pond in Lawrence Co. Indiana. I must have been in the water from the time I was a baby. My brother says he remembers when Dad was teaching him. He was very young. He said he was trying to swim and our Dad kept urging him on to swim just a little further. He was trying so hard and was moving his tired arms until he couldn't go any more. He let his feet down and said the water was only about a foot deep. He had been swimming for some distance and has been swimming every since.

The swimming pool was closed on Wednesday. So what did the gang do? We spend the day at the river. One of the gang was Roy Riggs, who lived on the river. His family had a large in-board motorboat and they allowed us to take it for the day. There would be ten or maybe twelve of us "river rats" spending the day going down the river to the Williams Dam. Someone was on the surfboard tied to the back of the boat all the ten miles down and ten miles back. We would stop and play in the water. One farmer had an old tire swing that was fastened on a limb out over the water. Of course we all took advantage of this play tool. We would take hold of the tire and pull it up on the hill. Then run and swing out over the river and drop in the running water. As I was hitting the water, I also hit something else. I think it was a big fish that hurried to get out of my way. It did not stay around to get my apology.

About the time we reached the Stump Hole Bridge, the hungry group would scramble up the bank and open up our picnic lunch. Phyllis Bowden and I always brought ham salad sandwiches made from boloney. We had put it together in the morning before the adventure down the river. We would add boiled eggs, pickle relish, onions and salad dressing with the ground up boloney. Teenagers have a wonderful appetite. I don't remember any of it left by the time our water adventure was over.

There was a power station at the Williams Dam. The gang would stop the boat and play in the water a little ways above the dam. One day I dived in and was out in the water past where I should have been. I could feel the pull of the water going into the turbines. I knew I could not turn around. If I did, my momentum would be lost and I would be swept into the machinery of the Power Station. I struck out across the pull of the water and made it to the dam. Pulling myself up and sitting on the concrete, I knew I was not going to swim back. My friends kept calling, "Come on back you can make it". I replied I was NOT going to swim back. I would stay out there the rest of my life before I would swim back. Fear had taken hold. I did not like the pull of the water on my body that was dragging me into the turbines. It was a very dumb decision to swim out there, but one of the wisest was the decision was not to swim back. The decision was made to bring the boat as close to the dam as they dared and throw me the surfboard. I caught the board that was tied to the boat. Then I was pulled from the dam and up the river to safety.

Another wise decision was not to tell my Mother.

Chapter 33 —
Dance Group

ONE OF THE FUNNIEST things that every happened to me. The time was around 1936. The schools did not have cheerleaders that were trained in acrobats, it was not a school activity. I belonged to a dance group that was considered to be a novelty. We were students of Mrs. Long's dance studio in Bedford, Indiana. It was a lot of fun and we traveled with Rudy Deering's band. We traveled many miles (no more than ten miles), usually making all the Alumna Banquets around Lawrence Co, such as Tunnelton, Needmore, Mitchell, Brownstown, PTA meetings and etc. We did dance in the Congress Hotel in Chicago at one time. That was a big, big thing.

All of these places had fancy stages such as four sections pushed together in the gym to form a stage. There were usually three girls, two older ones, Naomi Jackson and myself, one younger girl that was thrown around in an act of adagio. It was unusual to have an adagio team of all girls. Sometimes there were five of us.

Tunnelton stands out in my mind because of that stage. We were twirling around ever so graceful until I stepped on the center of that stage. The four parts separated and I fell through, all the way to the gym floor. This program was always good for a laugh.

There was the time in Needmore when we preformed on a regular stage, but it was very small. We were doing our thing of cart wheels, back bends, front-overs, tumblings, climbing on each other showing off our dancing skills. We were so graceful until one of our maneuvers hit the curtains and brought the curtain down. The audience came down with laughter, too. Oh, we were a sophisticated group.

But the crown of all our experiences was the time we were in the old Stocker school and performing for the PTA in a basement room. There were five girls that night and the finale was a pyramid, build by two girls with one girl on the shoulders of the first two and the smaller girl, Marge Taylor (now Mrs. Jim Torphy) on top. The pyramid was built in a hurry for a great finale. Marge hit the ceiling and of course threw the whole team off balance, down all of them came. Where was I? I was doing my thing in front of the pyramid. I was in the splits holding my arms out for the great applause. The whole pyramid landed on top of me. We had applause. The whole room couldn't stop laughing. We all joined in the merriment. That team had a good time. That team stayed together until the older girls graduated from High School in 1938.

Good memories.

Chapter 34 —
My Room

When I was a teenager, my room was beautiful. I can't say I always made my bed, but it was all mine. I was happy in it. Two big windows and the summer breeze came through and cooled the room. There was one nice clothes closet and the bed was an antique cherry four poster. Yes, it was beautiful. The walls were papered in red poky dots and the ceiling was papered in blue and silver stars. Now what more could a girl want? It was pretty to me.

It came time for me to leave home and go out into the world. How come my mother immediately changed the decor of my pretty room? When I came home to visit, I found my room in soft shades of beige. Now why would she change my color scheme? I had thought it was pretty. It is a good thing we are not all the same. The world would be very dull if that were true. It was very nice of my mother to let me have my own color scheme while I still lived at home.

Chapter 35 —
Regrets

I WAS FULL OF energy and excitement as I dashed out the back door headed for the swimming pool. The city pool was only one block away from where I lived. I spent most of my free time at the pool with all of my friends. I was eleven years old and life was fun. I was always excited to be on my way.

I stopped short, for there on the back porch was my dear grandfather standing by one of the post. He was in his seventies and had been a strong farm man. But here he was crying, my dear granddad crying. Life was not as good as it use to be. He had lost my grandmother just a year before and his health was not the strong, vigorous thing it once was His will to continue life was not very strong. His steps were slowing and his feet would shuffle instead of stepping out as they use to. His voice was also changing. His words were not coming out his mouth in the order he wanted them. It was only a short time until he would be confined mostly to a chair. There he would sit not knowing the world around him. I supposed now the doctors would have a name for it, but in 1931, it was just "getting old". I loved my granddad and seeing him like this hurt. I stopped and wanted to go to him and give him a big hug. I was embarrassed that my granddad was crying. I wanted to give him a hug and tell him I loved him, but I didn't. I turned away and hurried to the swimming pool. But it has stayed with me all the years of my life. I am now 90 years old and I think," Why didn't I take time to give him a hug". That is a big regret in my life.

Chapter 36 —
Learning to Drive

My sixteenth birthday! There is something magical about age sixteen. It is the transition between childhood and being an adult. Yesterday I was only fifteen and today I am sixteen. That means I am old enough to drive a car.

My dad, Chester Baker, told me "Come on you have to learn how to drive. I need you in the business". The business was Dad and Mother's Appliance store. Many things were sold on time, meaning many people bought things for maybe fifty cents to a dollar a week. It was to be my job to go out and collect. Times were hard in 1936 and people had a hard time meeting their obligations. But Dad was having a hard time meeting his obligations, too.

He had an old sedan of Roosevelt make. He also had a new 1936, half ton pick up truck that he delivered his merchandise in. Of course it was a red one and I loved it. All of his trucks were red. It was so easy to learn how to drive in that pick up truck. I could see the road very well, I am not very tall. There were two peddles, a clutch and a brake. The accelerator was on the right side of these two peddles. The clutch had to be pushed to the floor when I wanted to change the gear shift. The gear shift was to the right of my leg and could be moved into First, Second and Drive. The gear shift was a long metal rod that came out of the floor and had a round ball on the top that fit into a person's hand. It also had a Reverse. It took a little while to coordinate my left and right foot with the movement of the gear shift. But my Dad had a lot of patience. I was soon learning to push in that clutch and apply the brakes if I wanted to stop and not kill the engine. The clutch had to be pushed in and the gear shift put in Low or First to make a smooth start. At the car gained speed I had to push in the clutch and change the gear shift to second. More speed and then push the clutch in again and put the truck in High. Now I am sailing down the road. Many, many times I killed the engine. But over time I managed to have a smooth take off.

Our car was an old Roosevelt and was not as easily driven as the pick up truck. I am short of stature and I could not see out of it as well as the pick up truck. But I managed to conquer the beast. Again Dad's patience paid off. I was driving out west of the town of Bedford when we came to the little group of houses called Eureka. There is about at thirty degree turn in the road that goes back to Avoca. As I was making the turn, my foot went to the accelerator instead of the brake. What did the car do? It went over in the ditch. Dad didn't say anything. We got out of the car and he got in the divers seat and backed the car out of the ditch. I was embarrassed and started to get in on the passengers side. I thought that is enough for today. But not Dad, he said," no you are going to drive it home". I got back behind the steering wheel and we continued to drive. I told you he was a man of great patience. I never in his ninety two years did I ever hear him raise his voice at anyone. He was a very special Dad.

The day I took my first driving lesson was special in other ways. It was my birthday and when we came back to the house from a driving lesson in the pick up. I had a surprise waiting for me. When I went into the house the house was full of my many friends. Boys and girls were there to help me celebrate my sixteen years. How fortunate I have been to have such loving parents. Mother and my girl friend, Naomi, had planned it and it was a secret to me. Mother had a five galleon can of Ice cream for all of them to enjoy. Five galleons sounds like a lot of ice cream, but that hungry group could get rid of all of it. I remember the boys dipping the ice cream dipper into that big can and then putting the round dips of ice cream either on an ice cream cone or in a dish. Soon the whole five gallon was gone.

What a blessings it has been just to remember some of the things that happened to me when I was a lot younger than I am today. God has been very good to me.

Chapter 37 —
Summer Fun

I ENJOYED SCHOOL, BUT I always looked forward to summer vacation, too.

I lived only one block from the Thornton City Park. How very wonderful for me. I spent most of my time at the park. There was the swimming pool that I was in every day. Before the summer was over, there was always swimming races for the city to come and watch what we learned during the summer. We even had a canoe in the water and we would try our skill at paddling the boat. For some reason I always turned the boat over. I could never keep my boat upright. Then I learned the boat had some help form some one already in the water and under my boat. But the audience thought it was hilarious. I am not sure I did. But it was all in fun.

There were soft ball games that I participated in. One year we even had a donkey ball game for us girls. Now that was something. The city turned out to see the fun. We batted the ball while we were standing on the ground, but we had to get on the donkey and ride him to first base, that is if we could get him to go the directions we wanted him to go. He had a mind of his own. I can't remember whither the first baseman had to ride a donkey to go get the ball or not. I think he did. I just remember we had a lot of fun and the town had a lot of laughs. I hope the donkeys had fun, also.

I participated in track. I tried high jumping, but sure was not very good at it. I tried Shot Put and won first place in State. That is not like the school sponsored sport we have today. It was an invitational to a lot of cities to come together and have fun. I was taught how to hold the ball, make my turns to gain speed and turn loose of that metal ball at the right time. I was lucky. My ball went father than any of the other balls. That made me the State Champ. I even had my picture in the Indianapolis paper as I let go of the ball. I have a blue ribbon to prove my story.

The Parks department had a wonderful plan for the children. There was even a drawing class and a contest in the sand pit to sculpture something made of sand.

The sliding board was under the beech trees and when we were on top of the slide, we could touch the over hanging branches.

The teeter totter was always fun. But if one person decided to jump off and the other person was still on the board. Oh, how hard that other person hid the ground! There was other equipment, but I can not remember the names.

There was even a fish pond on the ground and we could watch the fish as they were swimming in their watery home.

There was always a story teller in the afternoon. She was one of the school teachers and spent part of the summer reading stories to the little kids. I enjoyed the stories when I was younger.

My days were taken up by the activities of the summer schedule at the park.

A lot of my evenings were spent at the skating rink just a few blocks from my home. Around and around we went on that slick floor. So, many of my friends were there and a good time was had by all.

My skin was naturally dark and by the time summer was over I was as brown as a berry. I lived in the out doors. I had chores to do at home, but I always managed to spend most of my time out side. I found it exciting. But when it was time for school to start, I found that exciting, also. I had summer friends and I had school friends. It was a fun time in my life.

Chapter 38 —
I'll Never Leave You Kids Alone Again

MOTHER AND DAD HAD gone to Louisville and had intended to be back by the time Bake and I got home from school. But they were late. My brother and I had the house to ourselves. I don't remember what happened but the two of us got into a fight. He was chasing me. We were out in the yard. I ran into the house and slammed the front door. He was close behind and his momentum kept him going and his arm went through the glass in the door. The artery in his wrist was cut by the broken glass. He began running through the house with blood squirting everywhere. I was four years older, about ten or eleven, and I knew I had to get the blood stopped. I started chasing him and finally got him down between the living room and dinning room. I was sitting on him and trying to get a tourniquet on his arm above the cut. I guess we were making so much noise that the neighbor, Frank Bowden, came to see what the commotion was. He took charge and put a real tourniquet on his arm. He got us into his Buick (early 1930) and took us to the doctor to have his arm sewed up. We were back home before Mother and Daddy came home from Louisville. She took one look at us and the house and said," I will never leave you kids alone again."

Chapter 39 —
First job

THIS IS MY SENIOR Year in High School (1938) and I am now ready to graduate. I also have a job for the summer. That is very special. Jobs were hard to find. There are two of us from this class that have jobs with the city of Bedford. We, Roy (Whimpy) Riggs and I, would be working for the Parks Department at the city swimming pools. Roy would be working at Otis Park swimming pool as a lifeguard. I would be working at Thornton Park swimming pool as cashier and bookkeeper. I would also be teaching swimming in the mornings at both pools.

I was very proud to be making all of Twelve dollars a week. That was good money in 1938. The girls that worked at the Dime Store made only Ten dollars. My hours may have been longer than theirs. I worked in the evenings and on Sundays.

The pool was closed on Wednesday. That is the day the people of the pools spent their time down on White River. We would take Roy's boat all the way from White River Bridge over road 37 to the Williams Dam. We were known as River Rats. We really loved the name. The surfboard that was pulled behind the boat with the in- board motor was in use all the ten miles to the dam and back. The boat was larger than the usual boats on the river. It would hold twelve or more kids from all ages. We were young and life was ahead of us. It was a wonderful life.

I saved all of my money for my first year at Indiana University. Money was hard to come by, but I had enough for my first year. My fee in 1938-39 was Fifty Dollars a semester. That did not include the price of room and board. That seems almost unreal at the prices they are today in 2010.

Yes, God has been good to me.

Part Five:

MOVING ON

Chapter 40 —
Moving On

THE SENIOR HIGH SCHOOL Prom is a wonderful time in a young girl's life. This tall, handsome, dark curly haired young man had asked me to go to the prom with him. Of course I said "yes". His name was Charles Gordon Reynolds.

The prom was held in the Bedford High School gymnasium. It is a magical time in our lives. We are leaving High School to go out into the world. What is ahead for us in this life? I didn't know at the time, but this young fellow was to change my life. In a little over a year I was to become his wife.

We both started college at Indiana University in the fall. I started in as a Math major and a minor in Physical Ed. At the end of the first semester I changed major to Physical Ed and my minor to Math. I had had some trouble with College Algebra. I understood it and got my credit, but it was not as easy as it had been in High School. In High School I had taken Freshman Algebra, Geometry, Solid Geometry and Trigonometry. I had not taken Advanced Algebra. That was a mistake. I needed it for College Math.

We both started the second semester. But it was not long before Charles had to leave school for a hernia operation. He did not return to College.

We were married June 25, 1939 at my home 1516 Sixteenth Street in Bedford. We were married in front of the big picture window in the living room. It was a very hot June day and it was before the time of air conditioners. The borrowed fans were everywhere. I had a beautiful, but simple long white dress that Mrs. Carson had made for my wedding. Charles was handsome in his new suit that he had worn to the prom the year before. Only the immediate family was present, but that meant three sets of grandparents, aunts, uncles and cousins. The Grandparents were my grandparents, Jacob and Nellie Colglazier,

Charles's Grandparents, Walter and Myrtle Reynolds and Noah Frazier and his second wife. The house was packed with these special people.

Our honeymoon was in Paris, Illinois. Yes, we can say we went to Paris, but we don't have to say it was just over the State line.

Charles was working for my dad, Chester Baker, who had an appliance store. Charles was always interested in radios. Soon after we were married he took a correspondence course in Radio. I remember him studying late into the night. He enjoyed this study and his love for radio stayed with him during his whole life.

His pay was sixteen dollars a week. We were buying our house for Fifteen dollars a month. It was a very nice house at 1616 Sixteen street. It was the original farmhouse for that part of Bedford. It had six rooms and a bath. There was a cellar for storage of canned goods. We did not have a furnace. We had a coal stove in the dining room for the whole house. There were sliding doors between the living room and dining room. We keep them closed to conserve the heat for the kitchen and middle bedroom.

I gave piano lessons for 50 cents a half hour. I had studied music for eight years. I had a good knowledge of piano. I did not have the natural ability to go with it. But I could start young people on their life of music.

Eleven months after we were married we were blessed with a wonderful son. He was born May 27, 1940. His name is Gordon Frazier Reynolds. Of course he was named after his dad. The Frazier came from his mother's maiden name. Today in 2010 he has been retired from teaching Biology in Seymour High School for forty years.

We also have another son, Jack Randall Reynolds, born October 30, 1945. He is a graduate of Purdue and has retired from Collins Company in Cedar Rapids, Iowa as an Electrical Engineer.

Chapter 41 —
War Years

WORLD WAR II WAS on and all young men were being drafted. Charles's number was soon to be coming up and he decided to enlist in the Navy.

We were buying our house, 1215 Gladstone Ave, Indianapolis on contract and we changed it to a mortgage. We felt that was the safest way to go to ensure the house would be ours when he came back from the service. Our payments were Thirty three dollars a month.

Charles left for Great Lakes on Gordon's birthday May 27, 1944. He would stay at Great Lakes for the entire time of his service. He operated the movie projector that was used in the training of the new sailors. His radio knowledge served him well.

I was left in Indianapolis for a short time and then my Uncle Wayne Guthrie, who lived in Chicago, invited me to come and stay at his apartment. He lived on the north side of Chicago just a few blocks from where the "L" stopped on its way back from Great Lakes. My Aunt Bertha, my mother's sister, had died just a short time before. Charles got in from Great Lakes every other night.

Uncle Wayne worked at nights and I had a little boy to keep quiet during the time he was asleep. There is so much to see in Chicago. The ride on the "L" was only ten cents. Gordon and I got out almost every day. We visited the museums and zoos. It was really a wonderful time to see Chicago.

I became pregnant and decided to come back to Indianapolis and our own home to wait for the birth of my second child. It was past time for the baby to come and I was as big as a barrel. The day was beautiful the last of October and I raked leaves all day. I was feeling good.

That night, I knew it was time to go to the hospital. Virginia, Charles's sixteen year old sister and her boy friend took me to Methodist Hospital for the delivery of my new baby boy. I think the car hit every rough spot in the road. I was very uncomfortable. I was sick in the elevator going to the delivery room. I was on a table in the labor room and the nurse decided to leave. I called her back and told her the baby was coming. She took one look and they put something over my face to put me to sleep. When I woke up I had a new little boy, Jack Randall Reynolds born on October 30, 1945.

Charles's parents telegraphed him at Great Lakes and told him the baby was here. They did not tell him whether it was a boy or girl. He did not know until the next day when he got leave from the Navy and came to Indianapolis to visit me and his newborn son. The weather had turned into winter and I remember when he came into my hospital room that his pea coat was covered with snow.

The war was nearly over and Charles was discharged from the Navy early in 1946. He was working for NAFI, (Naval Aviation Facility Indianapolis). He continued to work in the Engineering department for NAFI until his death December 27, 1972.

Chapter 42 —
Stung by a Wasp

LAWN WORK IS SUPPOSED to be a joy or that is what I have heard. After working for several hours, the last thing to be done was to clean out from under a rose tree. I was being very careful to avoid all the stickers as I picked up the dead limbs as they lay on the ground. It was a painful job if one of my fingers should hit one of the thorns. The day was hot and the perspiration was thick on my body.

Some disagreeable wasp decided to sting me in the middle of the back. Did he know I couldn't reach that spot? His poison went through my body immediately. My stomach didn't like it and up came whatever I had for lunch. I felt as if I could not make it into the house. With effort I made my way into the building and dropped onto the bed. Oh, how I wanted to reach that spot in the center of my back with my hand. I not only physically couldn't reach the hurt, I did not have the strength to try.

That is where I stayed the rest of the day, until my sons came home from school and my husband came home from work. I stayed in that bed. I don't know what the family had for supper, as for me I didn't care.

Chapter 43 —
Carnival

MY TWO SONS, GORDON and Randy and I set out for an evening of fun at Linwood Field. There was a carnival in town and it was only about four blocks from our house. Gordon was ten and Randy was five. We had no idea what the evening was going to be like. It was in Indianapolis and in a section of town where we knew a lot of people. Our church and school were also near and we would see a lot of people we knew.

Oh, what fun! We would try out the Merry Go Round, the Swings, and Midget Cars and of course the Farris wheel. Don't forget the Farris Wheel. There were two wheels to choose from. The excited boys and I paid our fees and scampered up into the seat that was held stead by the carnival men so we could get in. The bar came across our laps to hold us in place. As soon as we were buckled in, the men let go and the seat began to swing as the big wheel started to turn and then stop so the next riders could get into there seats. When all seats were full, the big wheel started to turn and pick up speed. What excitement we felt when we were on top and then the wheel would roll a few more feet and we felt like we were hanging over the precipice of a big mountain with the crowds of people below us.

With the laughter and screaming of the people something unthinkable happened. The Farris wheel stopped with a jerk and fell sideways. Everything was quiet. We were in the very top seat. The Farris wheel fell against the uprights that held the mechanism that makes the wheel turn. Thankfully that was strong enough to hold the big wheel and all its passengers. The carnival men began to run to the back of the big wheel and grabbed some kind of bar or rope. With all there strength the men started pulling and the wheel slowly started to right itself. As I looked down, I could see the straining muscles of those men. They were pulling with all their might in order to keep us alive. Inch by inch the big wheel finally came up right and started to roll. Very slowly, the wheel inched its way forward. The people were disembarking as their seat came to the landing. As our seat reached the over hanging precipice, it happened again. The wheel tipped to the left and was caught by the strong uprights. Again we were stranded with the wheel laying over sideways. Again those wonderfully strong men started the laborious task of pulling that huge Farris wheel manually. Again we inched slowly upright until the gears meshed and we were headed over and down until each and every one of the passengers were safely on the ground.

We were expecting an evening of fun and enjoyment, but not that kind of a thrill. God was with us. That Farris wheel was out of working order the rest of the week that the carnival was at Linwood Field. Although I later became an airplane pilot, I never rode a Farris wheel again.

Part Six:
EAST SIDE OF INDIANAPOLIS

Chapter 44 —
Warren Township, Indianapolis,

In 1953, Charles and I decided to build a bigger and better home on the outskirts of Indianapolis. We finally found a lot that we thought was promising. It was an acre and a tenth of tall weeds. Very few houses were around this area. We liked it. We liked the school system and that was important. Gordon would be starting High School and Randy would be in the third grade. It was a very good choice. We paid fifteen hundred dollars for the lot.

We had our house plans and our contractor. Soon the building was in the process of becoming our new home. I wanted a stone house. I had come from Bedford, Indiana which is the heart of the limestone industry. I wanted my new home to represent my history. The house had a living room, dining room, kitchen, bath and three bedrooms. It had a full basement and a big two car garage. It also had a nice fireplace. The man that built the fireplace bragged that he could make a fireplace that would heat the whole area and he did. It was a beautiful stone fireplace in the south wall of the living room. There were big sliding door closets in each bedroom as well as a coat closet in the living room. There was a large storage place in the dining room built over the stairway going to the basement.

The bathroom had a large closet and an opening in the bottom that let to a clothes shoot going down into the basement. The washer, dryer and ironing board were in the basement.

Charles had his area where he worked on his radios. He was a Radio Ham. He had his license to operate his Ham Radio and his call letters were W9ATE. He talked to people all over the world with his Ham Radio.

He also had one end of the basement for his model trains. He loved trains and spent many hours with his miniature models.

There was another house being built on the next lot at the same time. Wonders happen everywhere at any time. We did not know these people, but we soon learned that they were from the same area that we were from. She was from Mitchell and he was from Orleans. That is only ten miles south of Bedford. Their names were Bill and Barbara Stroud. Our parents knew each other. We became lasting friends. No one could have any better neighbors than we had.

At the back of the lot was a big forest with huge trees. It was beautiful. We also found as we cleaned off the tall weeds that who ever owned the lot before us had planted two rolls of all kinds of fruit trees. They were so small that they couldn't be seen in the tall weeds, but they had a wire fence around the base of each tree. They did grow when the weeds were cut and we had different kinds of persimmon trees, apples, pears, peaches, cherries and other kinds of fruit trees. They did not all survive, but many of them were there for us to enjoy.

We moved into the house on Randy's ninth birthday, October 30, 1954.

Our new address was 211 Delbrick Lane, Indianapolis.

Chapter 45 —
Starting to Work

I BECAME ACTIVE IN PTA (Parent Teachers Association). My boys were in school and I enjoyed my friendship with the other parents and teachers. I had been living in Warren Township for two years. I became acquainted with other people in the area.

The telephone rang a couple of weeks before Christmas break. It was Miss Siebert, Dean of the Girls and Manager of the Cafeteria. One of the women workers in the cafeteria had an emergency operation and would I help out. Of course I would and I did enjoy working with the other women.

Christmas came and went and another woman was out because of illness. Would I continue helping? Yes, I would continue working for the rest of the school year.

The school was in a renovation process. It was becoming larger. A new cafeteria was built with much more space and new equipment. Miss Siebert called me and wanted to know if I would take over the management of the dish room. Yes, I would and enjoyed it. The students could put their trays on the counter of a large window. From there the women could empty the trash on the trays and put the dirty dishes onto a conveyer belt going into the dish washer. Other women would take the clean dishes off the conveyer and stack them ready to use the next day.

This was a wonderful new innovation in school lunch. But there was more to come. The township was soon to build a completely new High School, Warren Central. The new school was much larger and the dish room became much, much larger. There were ten women working in the dish room as well as ten students. The dish washer was a huge mechanical monster. Two women worked on each end of the machine, two putting on and two taking off. The lunch trays were coming in on a conveyer belt. Women were busy removing the left over lunch items. The person at the garbage disposal was a very busy person. Nothing fazed her. She could take whatever the students choose to leave on their trays, even a live snake. She would dump the tray and down went the snake into the garbage disposal.

Some of our student workers were Special Ed people. They seemed to enjoy their job. I think they were proud that there was something they could do. It was a training period for them.

I stayed with the school for twenty six and a half years. I advanced with the school and the last few years I was the School Food Director for the whole township. When I retired in 1983, there were thirteen schools in the township.

Chapter 46 —
Blaze, Our Collie

GORDON GOT A PUPPY when he was three years old. She was a mixture of chow and bulldog. She became a very loving family dog and lived until he was a senior in High School. How fortunate we were to have this loving animal for his entire school years. Her name was JoJo.

Gordon found another dog to take the place of JoJo. His name was Blaze, our family collie. He was an outside dog and we loved him dearly, He had a blaze streak on his forehead when he was a puppy, but it had disappeared as he became older. We still called him Blaze. He was a very good dog to train. We had an acre and a tenth of yard that was not fenced. But the dog knew not to step over the boundary. But he was also a stubborn dog.

One of his bad habits was jumping on people. He was so very friendly. He wanted to greet people by jumping and putting his paws on that persons shoulder. Yes, he was a big dog. The book says the way to break a dog from doing this was to step on their hind feet. I tried that and all it did was to teach him to jump and then side step until I couldn't find where his feet were. Oh, yes, he was a smart dog.

He was an out side dog and wouldn't come into the house. His fur was thick and hours of brushing did not get all the loose fur out. When it was time to go to the vets, he was not happy. The vet was inside a building and he did not want to go into a building. I could get him to the door and force him inside and then he would sit down on his haunches and wouldn't go any farther. It is a good thing the floor was well waxed. He would sit there and I would have to push him or pull him across that floor with him in a sitting position.

With all his good training "come, sit, stay, roll over and etc", he had another bad habit, that was barking. He would bark at any thing and everything and nothing. At night he would bark for no reason, just because he liked to hear himself bark. I tried all kinds of things to stop his barking, but nothing worked. I would tell him "No" and he would stop and as soon as I went away he would start barking again. He was a loving dog and trying to teach him not to bark almost broke my heart. There came a time when I had a bucket of water in my hand and he started barking. I yelled "No" and threw the water in his face.

He stopped and looked at me and went into his dog house. Now this was a beautiful dog house that my husband had made. He took off a full week from work just to make this house. You can imagine the love he had for this dog. When the surprised shower hit the dog he went into his house and turned his face away from me and put his nose into the back corner of his house. He wouldn't look at me for over a week. I loved him and my heart was broken. When I would take food out to him he would go into his house and turn away from me.

About a week of turning away, he was ready to make up. When I took his food to him, he met me and put his paws on my shoulder and his long nose against my neck. It was so warm and soft. He was sorry he had behaved badly. He was giving me his love again. After that whenever he started to bark, all I had to say was a soft "no" and he would stop and not start again.

Do dogs have feelings? Indeed they do and they can return your love with all their doggy heart.

Chapter 47 —
Washington DC

DURING THE SUMMER OF 1958, Charles' job took him to Washington DC. He was the liaison person between NAFI and Washington. What a wonderful opportunity to visit our country's capitol. We had a government apartment just a few blocks from the west side of the south lawn of the White House. It was a very hot summer and the time before air conditioners. Much of our time was spent on the roof top garden. The roof garden was a place to cool off. It was both a playground and a place for socializing.

The boys left the apartment and were gone much of the day seeing the many interesting things in Washington. They did not feel "at risk" during the daytime. I knew they would be home by supper time.

Randy remembers the tracked trolleys and how relatively easy it was to get around since we lived right down town. He spent much of his time visiting the FBI building. They came to know him and would let him visit the shooting range. He came home with spent bullets they let him have. He also enjoyed the Smithsonian, the Art museum and many other museums. The Navy building has special memories for him.

Gordon spent much of his time in the roof garden working on a model of a P51 Mustang. He also had a special liking for the Smithsonian Museum.

We all climbed the Washington Monument and we took a boat cruise on the Potomac River.

We all remember the cooking smells coming from the other apartments. It seems that most everyone cooked with olive oil and garlic.

We did visit congress and watched the working government. It was a special time for all of us to remember.

Chapter 48 —
College years

BOTH OF MY SONS had a desire for education. Gordon graduated from Ball State University in 1963 and Randy graduated from Purdue University in 1968.

Both boys were married while they were in school. Gordon and Barbara Feuerbacher were married August 12, 1961.

Randy and Pamalie Wilson were married August 26, 1967.

Both boys liked music. Gordon played the accordion and Randy played the saxophone and bassoon. Randy played in the Marching band at Purdue during his Freshman year.

Gordon started at Purdue in Aeronautical Engineering. He had a job during the summer at NAFI in the Engineering department. This is the same place his dad worked. He was an outdoor person and did not like working all day in a building without any windows. After two years at Purdue he changed schools to Ball State University in Education. He was much happier there. I told Miss Siebert, my boss at Warren Central High School, that Gordon had changed his major. She said "I could have told him a long time ago that Education was the place for him, but he had to find it out for himself". Years later he retired from teaching Biology at Seymour High School.

Randy started in Electrical Engineer and stayed with it his entire life. He retired from Collins Company in Cedar

Part Seven:

GRANDDAUGHTERS

Chapter 49 — Special Joys

THE JOYS OF BECOMING grandparents are very special. From the very beginning when you first hold that wonderful bundle of God given joy and through out the rest of your life, things will never be the same. Something very special has come into your life. A person's thinking is different. That special child is in all of a person's thinking and doing.

Tara came into our lives while Gordon was still in Ball State University. She was born May 24, 1962. Barbara and Gordon were married August 12, 1961. There bundle of joy came within their first year of marriage. It was not easy, Gordon was working at two jobs as well as going to school full time. Charles, my husband and I, could only afford to pay his fees and books. He had to earn the money for his living quarters and food. But he had the desire for a degree in Education and worked to achieve that goal. Tara was at her daddy's University graduation.

His first job teaching was at Lapel. They lived in Anderson, Indiana.

Shannon was born March 5, 1965 while they lived in Anderson. It was winter and there was snow and ice on the ground. Gordon borrowed his younger brother's car so he would have transportation when that special day would come. The day came and another bundle of joy came into this world.

Gordon's teaching job moved from Lapel to Seymour, Indiana in 1967. There he remained until 1999 (32 years) when he retired from that school system.

There was a new Lutheran High school being built in Seymour at that time. He was asked to help them out by teaching Biology for them. He did teach there for four years

Chapter 50 —
Tara and Shannon

TARA AND SHANNON HAD a special place in our hearts. Their granddaddy, Charlie, loved little children. It was a joy to see them together. He was always picking them up and carrying them around. As they grew older, he would always have tootsie roll candy in his pocket to give them. When he cut the big yard he would attach the wagon on the back of the motorized lawn mower and let them ride in the back. They would cover themselves over with a blanket so the grass clippings wouldn't get on them. All three of them would enjoy the ride.

As Christmas was drawing near, the girls and I would write our letter to Santa Clause and then take the letter and put it in the fireplace and watch the flames change the letter to smoke and fly up the chimney. The letter was on its way to the North Pole and into Santa's work shop. We knew Santa would get our wishes.

On Christmas Eve we would look out into the star lit sky and watch for Santa's sleigh to fly through the heavens. The girls would get into their warm beds and try to stay awake so they could see Santa putting their toys under the Christmas tree. But sleep would over take them and they were soon in slumber land. The next morning would come quickly and there were their presents already under the tree. Santa came while they were asleep.

What wonderful memories.

Chapter 51 —
To My Granddaughters

GRANDDAUGHTERS, YOU HAVE ALWAYS been very special and you are still very special today.

I am very fortunate to have granddaughters with so much wisdom and love.

One of my memories, Shannon, is of you sitting astride a little toy on wheels and your little legs would go fast as you rode that scooter around the circle drive way beside your house. I can still see you in my mind as your legs would propel that small toy around and around.

Shannon, I remember when you would lay on the ground at the small fish pond in your back yard and play with the little turtles. Your mind was learning many new things.

I remember your doll house that the men in the family spent most of Christmas Eve night trying to put it together for Santa Clause to leave it in time for Christmas morning.

When you were little and you would come to my house to visit, what a wonderful time we had. We would read stories together and play on the piano. You would help me sat the table. When lunch was over, Shannon, you would get up from the table and head for the bedroom. It was time to take a nap. You would climb up in the baby bed and start bumping your head on the pillow and soon you would be asleep. No one ever had to tell you to take a nap, you just knew it was time.

Tara, you would snuggle up close to me and we would read a book and laugh. What wonderful hugs we had.

The three of us would sit around the fire place and watch the flames making all kinds of designs and let our imaginations work overtime.

You would go out doors in the winter time and skate on the little pond in the back yard. Do you remember the time you were playing on the ice and your dad and mom came out and your dad had a little puppy sticking her head out from his coat? I can still see you two running toward your dad and that puppy.

Do you remember how we would look up into the sky a few days before Christmas and wonder if we could see Santa's sleigh up there among the stars? How we would listen for his sleigh bells the night before Christmas? Do you remember how Jesus would listen to us as we said our prayers at night?

Do you girls remember singing together? Your voices were beautiful and blended in harmony. Do you ever sing together now?

Do you remember picking up persimmons in my back yard and how about the gooseberries? They sure had a lot of stickers on their bushes. How about the woods behind my yard? It was a place of wonder with all the wild flowers.

How about checking the stone in my house to see how many fossil we could find? The stone had been alive with creatures at one time. Both of you had many questions and I loved to try and answer them. I am sure I didn't know the answers to most of them, but I was happy that your minds were questioning things around you.

Both of you liked to go flying with me in my airplane. You were my best passengers. You would sit in the seat next to me and pretend to be flying the plane.

When you were little I would fly from Indianapolis to Seymour to give you piano lessons. I was not a very good pianist, but I did have a good foundation for the basic and could start you on your music. I do not know how long I did that, maybe a year. Then I felt you were ready for a real piano teacher. How proud I was when I attended your first real piano recital. You were both doing wonderful well. Shannon, you told me later that you did not know that my flying down there was special. You thought all grandmothers did that. I was happy when you continued with your music.

I remember when Tara got her first job in the little store on State Road Eleven. I was proud when I went in there and she would wait on me. Later she was a life guard at a swimming pool. I was happy that both of you girls were good swimmers. Water was a very much part of my life and I was glad you girls were caring it on. I came from a mother and father that were swimmers. I am sure they would be proud that their great, great granddaughters are caring on the love for the water.

Shannon, I was proud of you when I attended you gymnastic event and you were on the uneven bars. You did a wonderful job. You were so very graceful and beautiful.

Tara, I was very proud that you were on the varsity swim team all four years you were in High School

Your granddad would always bring you tootsies roll candy. He loved you dearly. You were the apple of his eye.

Do you girls remember combing my hair? I liked to have you comb my hair.

Did you girls think Grandmother had funny ides when I asked you if you would like to raft through the Grand Canyon? But you didn't hesitate to say "yes". We did have a good time. (Rafting with Grandmother)

Our good times have continues to this day. We are so very fortunate to have the relationship we have had and still have.

Shannon, you reminded me of another time that is in our memories. That is the time the three of us went to Washington Park Cemetery to feed the birds. There were big swans on the lake and for some reason one decided we were not there friend. Maybe it had some babies near by. It started after us at a fast run. It was big enough, that when it was out of the water, its head was on the same level with mine. The head was going back and forth as it ran toward us. It was coming fast. I got you girls behind me and stood my ground. It was the grace of God that I swung my purse at the head of that huge bird. The purse hit the swan squarely on the side of its head and the head was forced backward, one hundred eighty degrees. The swan left and we were safe.

Chapter 52 —
Grand Canyon

I WANTED TO DO something special for these girls for their High School Graduation. The gift was a rafting trip through the Grand Canyon. We spent nine days rafting from Powell Dam to Lake Mead.

Tara was eighteen and Shannon was fifteen. Our adventures are found in my book, "Rafting with Grandmother".

Chapter 53 —
College Girls

COLLEGE GIRLS! WHAT DO College girls think of when Spring Break is coming soon? 'Florida!'

What do grandmothers think about when their granddaughters are thinking of Florida? She is thinking, "How to keep them from going!"

Then some thinking took place. If the girls are wanting to go someplace and grandmother doesn't like the idea of Florida, how about someplace else. Sure, Hawaii sounds more exciting than Florida.

'Tara and Shannon, would you like to go to Hawaii on your Spring Break"? "Oh yes, Grandmother"

Plans were made and the time came when all three took off for the big adventure of Hawaii.

The memory if landing in Hawaii and the whiff of perfume floating upward from the millions of flowers to welcome a person to this island is a memory to remember always. It was an exciting week.

The girls remember the glass bottom boat and snorkeling in Captain Cook's Underwater State park. A person could look straight down thirty feet and see the white sand and the scuba divers doing their thing. The snorkelers were doing their thing near the top of the clear, clean water. That was what these three were doing. The girls were swimming with the fishes and feeding them with the wafers the captain of the boat gave his passengers. Small fish, big fish and fish of all the colors of the rainbows were everywhere. What a sight! Grandmother was doing her thing, too. She had wafers and the fish were coming to her. Then she decided to swim out beyond the reef and see what things were like out there. There was no bottom to be seen and the water was black and frightening. It didn't take long for her to get back inside the reef and more friendly surrounds. She might not have been so brazen if not for the fact she had been give an inner tube to make sure she stayed afloat. She did some fast kicking to get back inside the reef.

One girl remembers the macadamia farm. Having never tasted macadamia nuts before and the office had macadamia this, macadamia that and macadamia covered with chocolate for sale, the three almost made themselves sick just trying all that they could eat.

All three remember the volcano that had started to erupt the year before. The tour to the top of the volcano was always to be remembered. They walked on the crater where the steam was coming up beside each person. Little did they know that same volcano would still be erupting today, some twenty years later. The volcano was Kilauea. It is the home of Pele, the volcano goddess of ancient Hawaiian legends. The grandmother picked up some pieces of lava to take home with her. She couldn't understand why the guide was very upset. What he was trying to tell her was that Pele would become very angry if pieces of the volcano would leave the island. The motor trip around the island was to be stopped because the lava had come over the road and the road would be no more. The bus turned back to the starting point. But it was another day of adventure.

On the sailboat trip to the little island of Lanai, the Orcas whales followed the travelers. The group found the Killer Whales very friendly. With the clap of the hands, the whales would come to the top of the water and see what we wanted. It was a delightful day. The day was spent on the 'Pineapple Island' with a picnic on the beach and the day in the water. Grandmother had rented an underwater camera. With flippers on, the three tried to get through the waves near the shore. That is hard to do. Grandmother found herself thrown upon the sandy beach by the waves. Finally some men felt sorry for her and pulled her through the waves into the quieter water beyond the surf. Then the underwater camera was put to use. Shannon, one of the granddaughters came up beside the grandmother and said " Grandmother, there is a great big fish beside your feet". Grandmother naturally said, "here is the camera, take a picture." The grand daughter went under water and that picture proves the fish was almost as big as a person. No one thought about sharks at that time. The picture is a wonderful keepsake. One of the lessons learned was that volcano ground is like glass and will cut a person's feet.

Sunscreen is a must when a person is on the beach all day. But it must be applied several times. Grandmother made the mistake of applying it only once in the morning. Since she normally did not sunburn, she never thought to keep on applying it. That was a hard lesson.

The next morning was time to start back to the main land. She couldn't lean back against the seat of the airplane, because her back was so painfully burnt.

Shannon left the summer paradise to go back to the snow in Indianapolis wearing summer shorts. This was the last of February and wintertime. She did have a sweat suit she put on in Oakland, California, the stop over before the group headed back to Indiana. However, her feet were still in sandals and that is not the best foot wear for snow.

Part Eight:
GRANDSONS

Chapter 54 —
A New Generation

THE COMPANY RANDY WORKED for sent him all over the United States and even to Italy. He and Pam lived a number of different places in their early married life. His first job was with Crane Naval Base in Green County near Bedford, Indiana. He worked there seven and a half years and then moved to Collins in Cedar Rapids, Iowa. Both he and Pam started working for Collins at the same time. They were married fourteen years before their first child was born. The boy, Andrew, was born Sept. 27, 1981. Their second son, Alex was born December 27, 1983. I had two more grandchildren almost twenty years after the granddaughters were born. Each set was very special in their own way.

I remember going to Iowa that Christmas to stay with Andy while his mother was in the hospital. She had caught a very bad cold and was very uncomfortable. There was a lot of snow on the ground and we were wondering how we would get her to the hospital if we were snowed in. The baby did not catch his mother's illness. I remember the baby being in a little crib and his big brother, Andy, peeking over the side of the crib and looking at his new little brother. His eyes were big with wonder.

They lived on a farm near Center Point, Iowa. The boys grew up roaming the countryside. There was a grass runway for airplanes on this farm. Since I had my own airplane, I was able to fly to their farm in only about three hour from Indianapolis, Indiana. How fortunate I was to be able to see them often. These boys became very special to me, just as their girl cousins were special twenty years earlier.

Chapter 55 —
Farm Boys

THE BOYS LEARNED A lot from the farm. Their mother had a bee hive at the far end of the runway. That was a learning experience. They tried to help the man that tended the crops. They built a tree house. They ate grapes from the grape arbor. As they grew older they had a small motorcycle. They could use the runway for their riding. They built small hills of dirt so they could learn to jump the cycle.

Alex was the studious one and worked on his home work before he went out to play.

They spent part of each summer with me. I lived only one half of a block from the city swimming pool. Much of their time was spent in the pool. Andy helped a friend deliver papers here in Bedford. One day he came home from delivering papers and he had a little black puppy. The puppy had followed him home in his arms. He said, "Grandma, can I keep him". I told him he would have to ask his parents. Of course they said "yes". We named him "Inky". He was a black lab. The puppy had been on its own for some time. His collar was embedded into his neck skin. We removed the tight collar and I am sure the doggy felt better. We found out he was being fed by a restaurant down town. Where he came from we never found out. They had that puppy until the boys were grown men.

Since both parents worked, there had to be a place for the boys during the summer. By the time they were eight, they were in summer camp. Andy was in Chinese Camp. It was sponsored by Concordia University. It was a fun learning experience. They were not to bring any contraband into camp with them. Contraband was anything in English. From the time they went into camp, everything was in Chinese. Andy became fluid in Mandarin Chinese. He could read, write and speak another language. He attended Chinese camp for eight years.

Alex chose a German camp to spend his time. What a wonderful opportunity for young people to learn a second language. Alex, from the time he was a preschooler until present time wanted to be a doctor. There was only one time during his youth that he wasn't sure. That was the time he fell out of the tree and broke both arms. He spent some time in the hospital and after he got out he had to have help doing the normal things a boy does. He was in grade school and he had to have an older boy take him to the bath room. However, breaking both arms probably saved his head from being broken. The desire to be a doctor stayed with him. Now in 2010 he is in his fourth year of Medical School in Des Moines, Iowa.

Chapter 56 —
Precious Grandsons

WHILE HAVING THE OIL changed in my car at Good Year Garage, I decided to send the two boys, Andy and Alex, across the street to the Midtown grocery. I gave the boys a twenty dollar bill and told them to get some fruit.

They were gone for sometime and when they returned they were caring a huge watermelon. They also had a large sack of groceries. They had bought a lot of various kinds of fruit. Their bill came to $20.02. They lacked the two cents having enough money to pay for it. They found a penny in the parking lot and a man gave them another penny. They had $20.02, just enough to buy their groceries. Their faces were so proud when they came across the street with their purchases.

Precious Memories

Chapter 57 —
Graduation Gift

IT WAS NOW TIME to think of a High School graduation gift for the boys. I had taken the girls rafting through the Grand Canyon. [My book, 'Rafting With Grandmother']. What could I do for the boys? I decided on a trip up to the tundra at Churchill, Manitoba, Canada. The boys got permission from their school to be gone during the first week in November. Heavy clothing was obtained. We lived with the polar bears for a week. Dog sledding was very important. The northern lights were fantastic. It was a wonderful adventure. [My book, "Grandmother's Adventures]

Chapter 58 —
Sleeping With a Pit Bull

WHEN A GRANDMOTHER GETS to visit both grandsons, who are in different colleges, on the same day, then it becomes a very special time.

I left Bedford at 8:15 A.M. and drove to Cedar Rapid, Iowa and arrived about 5:30 P.M. By 7 P.M. less than twelve hours after I left Bedford, I was seated in the jump seat of a pick up truck with Randy, my son and his wife, Pam and also the dog. The truck was pulling a small Nomad Camper. We were headed to Ames, Iowa to visit my grandson Alex that is in college at Iowa State. He has a job for the summer at the Chemistry Dept. It is a wonderful visit.

The next morning we took off for Sheldon, Iowa to visit the other grandson, Andy, who is in Sheldon, Iowa Community College. It is a four and half hour drive. His school does not get off for the summer. It goes around the calendar. He is taking Heavy Equipment and learning not only how to operate but also how to work on them. They have special jobs for the summer. We were to help him move from one house to another and were there for three nights, staying in a very nice campground. The dog belongs to this grandson. She is a Pit Bull and I know they have a very bad reputation, but she is a very gentle, but a very stubborn animal. The camper is small, but it did have a bathroom and a full size bed. My bed was made by letting the table down until it was level with the seats and then using the cushions for a mattress. It really was very comfortable. The dog slept on the floor or she was supposed to. That is until one night she decided to sleep at the foot of my bed. It was cold that night and she is a short haired dog and she started to shiver. Her shivering woke me up so I took this opportunity to make a trip to the bathroom. When I came back the smarty dog had not only moved to my pillow but was also under the covers. She pretended to be sound asleep. I knew she was trying to fool me. I tried to move her, I pulled and I pushed. She acted like an inanimate object. She thought

I would think she was just a rock and couldn't be moved. I thought, "Buster, you are not going to get the best of me". I started kicking that hunk of a hound. She was not a large dog, but she was forty five lbs. of all muscle. There was no way she was going to move. The kicking did nothing. Finally, out of desperation, I laid down on the edge she had left me. She didn't like my body laying over on her and she moved over about an inch. So, I moved over on her again and she moved over some more. That is the way I finally found room enough to sleep. She seemed satisfied also to have a place to stay warm. That is my story of sleeping with a Pit Bull.

Part Nine:
SNOWMOBILE

Chapter 59 —
Snowmobiles in Yellowstone Park.

DID YOU EVER WONDER what Yellowstone Park looks like in winter? BEAUTIFUL!

My niece, Nellie and her husband Ralph, who are experienced snowmobile riders, my granddaughter Shannon, age 20, who could conquer any thing and myself age sixty five who had never been on a snowmobile before were taking a guided tour of this beautiful park.

This was to be three days of excitement. The first day, because it was a beautiful day and the sun was shinning, we were to tackle the mountains west of the park. West Yellowstone, Idaho was our head quarters at 6500 feet. I was prepared with the snowmobile overalls, boots, gloves and helmet that were given us. The people were divided into three groups according to their experience. I should have been in the beginners group, but my family did not want me to be separated from them and they said I could make it in the more experienced group. Little did they know! I did not realize how big that snow mobile was until I was seated on the monster. It was huge and powerful. We started out to climb the first mountain. Over the pristine snow we went. Wheee! I couldn't understand why the pine trees were so small. Then it was explained to me that these little trees were really over thirty feet tall and we were only seeing the tips of them. The snow was deep and soft. I was to learn the hard way.

I had reason to be thankful the snow was so soft and fluffy. It wasn't long before I turned my snowmobile over on top of me. They were all going so fast and I was a beginner. Of course all of them stopped and ran to help. Ralph was the closest and I yelled at him to take a picture. He said that was the first time he ever tried to help a person and they wanted their picture taken before he could help them. The snow was so soft and turning the snowmobile upright and me climbing out was not easy. The men finally got the machine righted and I tried to climb out. I had to crab craw very carefully in order not to sink deeper. I am sure it was not very graceful. That was only the beginning. I turned it over three more times before the day was over. What did they expect from a beginner? The road up the mountain was steep and with many hairpin turns. Since I was a beginner I did not keep my speed up in order to make the turns and over I went. I always leaned toward the mountain and not over the bank as an experience driver would. This mountain was 8000 feet tall. The top of the mountain was a picture of 'make believe'. The trees were frozen in all kinds of shapes. The wind had pushed them into fairyland phantoms and the snow had formed them into a frozen fantasy,

The high altitude was affecting me. I was very tired, but what my eyes saw was beyond explaining. We started back and I was going to be glad to get into my motel room, but no, we were then to conquer the next mountain of 10000 feet. Up we went. Near the top, it was so steep that many snowmobiles couldn't make it. I didn't try the last part. Many of the other people didn't either. Their machines would not climb. Down we came with still more to explore. The guide knew I was very tired and asked me if I wanted to go back to the village instead of staying with the group. Of course I did. This old granny couldn't take it. He said we were not very far from West Yellowstone and explained how I was to get back. I was to go straight and when I got to the power station I was to keep going straight and not turn. I started off. I had not gone far until Shannon and Nellie caught up with me. They did not want me to go alone. The guide didn't tell them about going straight at the power station and they turned down what looked like a path. They were so far ahead of me that I couldn't yell and tell them they were on the wrong trail. I followed them and then we came to a place where we could go no farther. We came to a high way and it was at least thirty feet below us. The road had been kept open by the highway department from the beginning of winter. We were actually above the information signs that were over the road. So we took off through the forest and were soon lost. Or at least I was. I kept going around and finally got my monster stuck in the snow. There was no way I could get out. I was beyond caring for that big overgrown hunk of torture. I was just going to forget it. I told the girls I was going to slide down the snow bank to the road and walk home. That was some snow slide I experienced, thirty feet straight down. I could see the town down the road. Not too far, if I wasn't so tired. I trudged on and tired to put one foot in front of the other one. My family was concerned and finally followed me. How they got those snowmobiles down that bank, I do not know. They had my snowmobile free and brought it to me. I climbed on and they went back after their other machine. I went on into this huge town of about four blocks square and got lost. I could see where I wanted to go, but couldn't get there from where I was. Big snowdrifts were everywhere. A man in our group found me, got on my machine and took me back to my motel. I would be so thankful for his concern and his help getting me back to where I could rest. My room was on the second floor. But how was I going to make it up those stairs? I started. The last few steps were painful. I was crawling. I don't think I have ever been so tired. In my room the bed was a place to drop and stay. Stay until I begin to get back to normal. This was the first of three days exploring the area.

The next day was a new start with renewed energy. I am a morning person so I took a walk early in the morning. It was fantastic. The moisture in the air had frozen into tiny crystals floating everywhere. The sun was shinning on these minute diamonds. I would reach out to touch them and there was nothing my hand could feel, another one of God's miracles.

I was smarter the next two days. Instead of riding the snowmobile, there was the Snow cat. It is a machine with tank treads for wheels. Wonderful! I saw the park from the comfort of a bus. The top was open and the passengers, about six of us, were able to stand up and look out at God's Glory. I did not have to worry about that hunk of metal that I had tried to conquer the day before. Herds of buffaloes would travel in the middle of the roads. The animals had the right of way. The snow cat had to wait until the buffalos would leave the trails. It was easier for the animals to travel in the roads than in the forests, so naturally they would be in the road.

For two days I enjoyed the mountains, animals and birds that congregated near the hot springs and many, many water fountains. The hot springs were deep and clear even as the water was boiling. Our eyes could look down into the center of the earth. There were many waterfowl that were wintering in the warm waters of the hot springs. The bison and elk were everywhere. I saw a wolf running across the trail.

Even under the snow, the ground could be hot to touch. The park is the crater of a huge volcano.

The rest of the family took their snowmobiles and toured Yellowstone. It is a fascinating place, and in winter it is as wonderful as it is in the summer. How thankful I am that God has allowed me to experience so many of his wonders. This is one of many.

Part Ten:
ISLAND HOME

Chapter 60 —
Island Home

MOST OF FOUR GENERATIONS of my family have been blessed with the opportunity to spend part of each summer on an island in Canada. It was owned by my mother and dad with two other couples. The five acre island was in Cedar Lake. It was about two hundred miles north of International Falls, Minnesota. They owned the south half of the island. We had a cabin in our part. There was a cabin on the north side of the island. However, it was seldom occupied.

When they bought the cabin in approximately 1955, it had two bedrooms, kitchen and living room. My brother and one of his friends build on another bedroom and put a porch on the east and south side of the building. There was no electricity or running water. Our water came from the lake. A water pump pumped the water into a holding tank on top of the cabin. From there it flowed into all three bedrooms and the kitchen. Our filtering system was a women's silk stocking. That kept all the undesirable things in the lake from getting into our drinking water. Yes, we drank right out of the lake.

We had the usual outhouse. Our heating was a wood stove that looked like a steam engine on a railroad. A big log could be put in at one time. It would heat the whole cabin in a very short time. One of the things the boys learned was how to split wood.

It was a beautiful and serene place. The trees were huge. Most of them were pine. We couldn't go to the store every day. We tried to go into the town of Dryden once a week. It was a town sixty miles from the island. We fished and ate fish every day. My favorite fish to eat is a Walleye. We did have a bottle gas stove and refrigerator.

Listening to the loons calling to each other was a special treat. The bald eagles would be nesting near by. The bears would come up in the afternoon to eat the clover that my mother planted in the yard. The bears paid no attention to us and we did not bother them. We just watch as they enjoyed their meal. They would also eat our blue berries on the west side of the island. Many different kinds of ducks would nest on the island. It was a wonder land of animals and birds.

There was a little inlet that we used for a boat dock. But we had to compete with a beaver to keep it open. The beaver wanted the same place we wanted for our boats. He kept building and we keep putting our boat in this inlet. Finally the beaver would slap his tail on the water and go some place else.

There was always a lot of maintenance to do every spring. There was one tree that we tried to straighten up and keep it growing straight. Ropes were tied to three sides of it so it could grow the way we wanted it to go. When we came back to the island in the spring, the tree was laying on the house. The beavers had decided they wanted it and had cut it off near the ground. However, they couldn't untie the ropes, so the tree was left where it fell when they chewed into the base.

Three young girls of the family were caught in the outhouse with a bear between them and the cabin. They were two sisters, Cathy and Mona Baker and their friend Donna Gering. When they saw the bear they did some loud screaming and the bear left. They could then come back into the safety of the cabin.

We tried to grow a garden and we put our garbage into the ground that we tried to cultivate. One thing that was very successful was rhubarb. The rhubarb grew very big and tinder. We ate it almost every day. It was especially good.

The darkness of the night was short. It would be almost midnight before we could go out with our flashlights and hunt for night crawlers. But night crawlers we had to have in order to go fishing. We would gather about two hundred night crawlers in an evening and they would last us for maybe two weeks. Bass, northern pike and walleyes were our main source of food.

Randy and Alex would scuba dive off the south end of the island.

The boys were good fishermen and they could clean their catch. The cleaning table was near the dock. They tried to get in early and get their fish cleaned before the mesquites started in just before dark. The mesquites were big and their bite would itch uncomfortably.

Many card games would be played in the evening by the light of a coal oil lamp.

There was electricity on the main land and there was a laundry mat at the end of this large lake. We would go down there and do our laundry and bring the clothes back and hang them on the line to dry. We also had a scrub board and used it part of the time.

The back porch was screened in and we could sit out there and watch nature, relax and not have to worry about the mesquites.

Chapter 61 —
Duck Family

I AM SITTING ON the high bank above the water. The lake is about fifteen feet below me. There is movement everywhere, in the sky, on the ground and in the water. A mother duck and her babies draw my attention. Something is wrong. She and the babies are hurrying one way and then change directions and hurry in another way. Then I see why. Something in the water is following them. All I can see is the back of some animal. It really looks like a big stick. I do not know what kind of animal is under that back bone. It changes directions with the path of the ducks. Oh, Please, don't let that thing catch those baby ducks.

Some one else is also watching the activity. Poppa duck is guarding his family. The big duck flies at that stick and the animal in the water has to veer away from the directions momma duck is going. But soon Poppa duck has to gain attitude for his next dive.

The thing goes after momma and the babies again. Poppa duck is more exacting this time and the animal is forced toward the island where I am sitting. As he comes out of the water, I can see it is a mink. He runs along the ground at the edge of the water. This takes him directly under where I am sitting. He doesn't take time to look at me. He is to busy dodging Poppa duck as Poppa is still diving toward him. Momma duck takes her brood to the west side of the island and to safety. There is always activity in nature.

How fortunate I am to be able to witness this activity.

Chapter 62 —
Animal Heart aches

OUR ISLAND HOME IN Ontario, Canada was a beautiful and restful place. It has a life of its own. My brother and his family and my family had the privilege of many hours of listening to the birds and animals and seeing the wonderful lake that went for miles.

My son and his wife and I were slowly boating around the five acre island and just enjoying the beauty of the far north. A mother duck took this time to bring her new babies from the nest to the water. There was a bank of about three feet. The mother duck jumped and the little ones followed after her. We stopped the boat and just watched. There are flaws in natures, just as in everything else. One little duckling turned upside down in the water. The mother went to its rescue. She took her bill and caught hold of the little one and flipped it up in the air hoping it would land right side up. But each time the little thing would turn over and go upside down. We were hoping her frantic effort would be successful. But no, it didn't matter how many times she flipped it up in the air. It always came down the wrong way. It was soon lifeless. There was no hope for the little duckling. Then the mother gathered the rest of her brood and swam away for the heart ache area.

My son picked up the drowned little bird and threw it way back in the trees. It would be food for some other animal. It would not be where the distraught mother could see it.

How thankful I am that God has allowed these eyes to see the beauty of His creations. The island home has some very, very good memories. Thank you, God.

Part Eleven:
LIFE CHANGING

Chapter 63 —
Life Changing

My life suddenly changed. I had been married for thirty three years and now I am a widow. Charles died suddenly from a heart attack. One moment he was with me the next moment he was gone. On December 27, 1972 I was sitting in the front room writing thank you notes for the presents I had received at Christmas. We lived in Indianapolis and most of our family lived in Bedford, Indian. Charles walked into the room from the kitchen and said, "I have the most awful pain in my chest". I continued writing the words "Bedford, Indiana" before I looked up. When I did look up, he was gone. He had let himself down on the sofa and his head was leaning back into the Christmas tree. He was gone. HE WAS GONE.

At first it is hard to believe. Then realty takes hold. I believe that God puts us in shock for several weeks after something like this happens. It allows us to do what every we have to do. I was fortunate I had two wonderful sons and their wives to help me over this disaster. I was also fortunate to have a good job. I was the Food Director for Warren Township in Indianapolis. It made me get up in the mornings and go to my job. It was a job that I liked. I liked the people I worked with.

The world keeps on turning and life keeps on going.

Chapter 64 —
Getting Lost

ABOUT TWO MONTHS AFTER my husband died, I was attending a Church Circle meeting in Beech Grove, Indiana. It was late when the group broke up and I started driving home to the east side of Indianapolis. Sherman Drive, which is the usual way from Beach Grove to the East side of Indianapolis, was being rebuilt. The night was dark and I tried to read the street signs and find a new way home. It seems I was going around and around. I would come up to the same dead end at Sherman Drive and have to turn around and go back to some where and see if I could find another route. I am not a cry-baby, but I begin to cry. I think it was the first time I had actually let down and bawled since Charles had been gone. I cried and cried and tried to drive. My thinking was," It doesn't matter if I get home or not. There is no one there to miss me". I was having a good 'pity party'. If my car just kept going off the ends of the earth, it wouldn't matter. No one was home waiting for me.

After what seemed like a long time, I came to a boulevard that I recognized. This led me to Washington St and Road 40. I knew my way home from this point. It was after midnight before I came to my home on Delbrick Lane.

In bed, with the covers over my head, I could cry myself to sleep. Oh yes, the Pity Party was in full swing. I could just forget about the rest of the world. It didn't care about me. It didn't matter what the rest of the world was thinking. There wasn't any one to care.

The next morning, God make me think. I had so much to be thankful for. I had a good job that made me get up in the morning and go to work I liked my work. I had good health and two wonderful sons that cared a lot and would always be there to help me. I had a nice home. God was helping me straighten out my thinking. I had wonderful neighbors and Church friends. All right get hold of yourself. The decision was made to never let this happen again. I was never going to get lost again. All roads lead somewhere. There is always a way back.

Sunday afternoon, when the traffic was light in the big city, I started out driving. I would drive every Sunday afternoon for several months. I was going to learn where all the roads went in this State Capital. I have never been lost again. I may not know for sure where I am, but I am not lost. ALL ROADS LEAD SOMEWHERE.

Even today, I like to take the back roads and find out where they lead. I like to go a different route to get to where ever I am going. ALL ROADS LEAD SOMEWHERE. Never forget that. There is always a way back home. That has become one of my mottos.

Chapter 65 —
Never Alone

THE SHOCK OF LOSING a spouse can be intense. Loneliness can overwhelm a person. However, God lets us know we are not alone from the beginning if we will be still and know that He is our Savior.

Loneliness was taking over my whole being that morning after his death during the Christmas season of 1972. As I closed me eyes, the loneliness continued to creep into my soul and again I found myself in disbelief that I had suddenly lost my husband of 33 years. The night before last he had died under the Christmas tree.

I looked out the dining room window and saw two little rabbits playing in the cold, crisp Christmas air. They were so much alive and having so much fun chasing each other around a tree and then jumping up in the air and turning around and chasing the other one for a while. They were telling me something. They were very much alive and life was not over for me nor neither was life over for Charles. He has left this beautiful Earth, but his joy of living was continuing. . He had only gone into another life of more beauty. He and God would remind me of this many times in the years ahead. God lets us know we are never alone if we will but be still and listen.

It has been two weeks since the death of Charles. I was not going to feel sorry for myself and I decided to work and obtain my aviation instrument rating. I had received my pilot's license the year before. The Instrument Rating was something I wanted. It was intense work and I did not have time to feel sorry for my self. My instructor, Jim Jackson, was exacting and made me work and work. I was to listen to the controllers, do what they say, keep the plane level, coordinate the rudder and yoke, watch the altitude, look out for other planes, watch my speed, don't let a wing dip, keep the nose on the horizon, practice over and over again. Why couldn't he just let me learn one thing at a time? No, it all had to be done at the same time. It was work, but the sky was friendly. I never felt alone even if I was practicing without my instructor. I was accomplishing what I wanted. I was playing in the sky. I was maneuvering my Cessna 172 and making it do what I wanted. It was not in charge of me. I was in charge of it. I was very comfortable in that left seat. I did not feel alone.

As the days flew by there was more proof I was not alone. Many things happened in that house on Delbrick Lane in Indianapolis, Ind. Things would move around apparently by themselves. Never was it frightening. The feeling of someone else was comfort. There was a time when a picture fell from the end table. I picked it up and put it far back from the edge. Half an hour later it was on the floor again. Again I picked it up and wondered how in the world it ended up on the floor for the second time.

There was a time I was awakened in the middle of the night by the sound of my jewelry box playing music. It was a box that Charles had given me. My heart beat inside my chest as I listened to the tinkle of the familiar sound. The box continued to play a few bars of music, I lay perfectly still, but was not afraid. After a few minutes, the music stopped indicating the drawer had been closed. I smiled to myself and then turned over and went back to sleep. A few weeks later the music box played for my son, Gordon and his wife, Barbara, as they were using the bedroom for the night.

The bathroom had its share of unusual happenings. I was taking a tub bath, when my eyes were directed toward the water controls. One of them was turning by itself. The shower came on and the water came out and gave me a good soaking. The shock of an unexpected drenching brought a shout from my lips, "Charles, cut that out". The handle again turned the water off and with no help from me. Why did the water come on? Why did I yell my husband's name? I was not thinking of him. The subconscious being is strong.

I started dating one of Charles's friends a few months after his death. At first it was a few dinner dates and an occasional double date with friends. My house had a little over an acre of yard to take care of. It also had many trees. I called my new friend, Frank, a frustrated farmer. He had been born and lived on a farm before he went into the Air Force for World War II. He enjoyed working in my yard or maybe he just liked to operate my John Deer Lawn Tractor. He lived in Greenwood, about a half hours drive to my house on the east side of Indianapolis. Many days he would be working in my yard early in the morning and continued working while I was at work. I worked in the school system of Warren Township as a School Food Director. He had retired from Naval Avionics, the same place my husband had worked. He wanted to put in a garden. I said, "Yes, I will cook the vegetables, but I will not can them". He always had a beautiful garden. He worked that yard for thirteen years until he, also, died of a heart attack.

Our friendship developed into a closer relationship. One night as he was putting his arms around me the telephone rang. I answered it, but there was no one on the line. He started to kiss me again and the telephone rang again with the same results. No one was there. What was going on in Frank's mind? I do not know. I thought it was funny. He left and went to his home. I couldn't keep from laughing, I guess that wasn't very nice of me, but I still think it was funny. What does that say about me? The next day he was back trying to make up some reason why the telephone would ring at that special time. He had some really far out excuses for the unexplainable.

I was never alone. Many more unexplained things happened. The lights would go off and on at odd time. Charles was an electrical engineer. None of this was frightening. The feeling of comfort was always there. I was not alone.

Part Twelve:
FLYING

Chapter 66 —
Flying Desire

I DID NOT REALIZE so many incidents in my life had to do with my passion of flying. But there is a correlation.

I am going back in time of 1925. This little girl of five was watching the skies as she continues to do even to this day. This has always been a great pleasure of mine to watch the sky and see the beautiful clouds and dream of playing in the white fluffy air.

This evening an object came in sight and to me it looked enormous. It was the Shenandoah, one of the experiment dirigibles the government made after World War One. Lighter than air was a thing of interest. This little five year old girl was standing beside the cistern pump looking up at this wonder. It was low enough to the ground that I could see lights in the windows. It must have been nearly dark because I could see the windows lit up. That light was a wonder. We had coal oil lamps in our house and I didn't see how they could be carried in the air and give such brilliant illumination. Electricity was not in my understanding. In my memory that was the last flight the Shenandoah ever flew. It seemed to me to be floating in the air. In September of 1925, in Cincinnati, the Shenandoah was ripped apart during a thunderstorm and 14 men were killed. Two of the men were Indiana University students.

In the year of 1928 the wonders of flight was coming to the public in the form of Barnstorming. World War one had opened up the sky to the inquiring public. War Aces were earning their living by flying from one farmer's field to another farmer's field and taking people for rides. Mitchell, Indiana had a grass field just north of town. It even had a hanger with a rounded roof so the airplanes could be kept out of the weather. This building is now a fire station.

How wonderful that this eight year old girl had grandparents that lived across the road from this wonderful activity. The road was magic in itself. It was called Dixie Highway. It was the main road between the south, Louisville, Kentucky and the north, Chicago, Illinois. The State called it Road 37. The summer was warm and the family would sit on the front porch watching all that was going on across the road. Of course curiosity would get them to decide to walk across the road and go for a ride in the Ford Tri-Motor airplane. The Ford Motor Company had built airplanes after World War One. What a wonderful experience. About eight or ten of the family would experience the thrill of a lifetime and climb into the magic carpet and take off into the wild blue sky. The ride was smooth, so smooth that this eight year old girl could not tell when the plane left the rough ground or when it landed. She always remembered that magical feeling of leaving the earth and going into the skies. The special pilot was a Mr. Redfern, a World War One Ace. The thrill of flight was beginning to form in this little girl's desire.

In 1939, soon after I was married, my husband, Charles Reynolds, arranged for me to take a ride in a small airplane at the Bedford airport. I do not remember who the pilot was, but I do remember I never said a word on the entire flight over the city of Bedford. It was magic to look down on the little houses and city stores that I knew so well when I was on the ground. Now, I could see the whole town at once and enjoyed each street that I had walked so many times. I enjoyed the big holes made by the quarries where the stone was taken out to build so many government buildings in Washington D.C. and other places across the country. I was so disappointed when he started back to the airport. I supposed he thought I did not enjoy it because of how quiet I was. That was not true. I was speechless with delight.

Charles always wanted to fly. He took flying lessons on the GI bill after he came home from the Navy. I would wait for him on a bench and watch the planes come in and fly out. I never became board. I was watching the activity going and coming from the air and also enjoyed looking for four leaf clovers in the grass. I still find my share of four leaf clovers every year. I do not remember a year that I did not find the lucky green plant. I enjoyed every minute. After he got his license and we had bought a plane, he encouraged me to take lessons.

His family had a history of dying at fifty- two. He wanted me to know how to get the plane down if he should die while flying the airplane. I enjoyed my lessons very much and the day came for me to fly solo. This is a special time in anyone's life when they take that flying machine into the air by themselves. There is excitement in every part of a person's body. My husband knew it was about time for that big day, but he did not want me to know he was concerned. But as I came into the airport after my first time by myself, I saw him peeking around the corner of the hanger. I knew he was there. I made my three solo landings that were required in my training. I received my license in June 1972 at the age of 52.

My husband was also 52 and what he dreaded also took place. He died of a heart attack that December. I know I used my flying as therapy. I went into Instrument training two weeks after his death. It was advanced flying and something I wanted and loved. It would occupy so much of my time I did not have time to feel sorry for myself. It is a wonderful feeling to be up in the sky and flying in and out of the clouds. I never felt alone when I was maneuvering "My Baby". That is what I called my Cessna 172 airplane. I knew someone was always with me. For the next twenty years flying was a big part of my life. I thank God for being with me and giving me the privilege of learning a little more of His Universe. It was and still is a very satisfying feeling. I am thankful for all the things He has allowed me to do and see.

Chapter 67 —
Flying

MY LIFE HAS BEEN divided into sections. Flying was a big part. I flew my soloed November 13, 1971 and sold my airplane the summer of 1988. Those were good years and certainly were a lot of fun. Many stories could be told about those years. My two granddaughters were my best passengers.

My daughter–in–law, Pam, who is also a pilot was going to fly the Powder Puff Derby as a copilot with Emily Earlywine. This was to be the last year for the Derby. The race was very well known and had a lot of prestige. It was a speed race from Sacramento, Calif. to Wilmington, Del. I was enjoying my new instrument rating and decided to fly to Californian to see the start of the race. Then my brain began to work. If I were going to fly out there and back, why didn't I enter the race? I had the requirements, I was an instrument pilot and I was a member of the Ninety Nines an International Organization of Women Pilots. It took a while to get all the papers in order and I chose my co-pilot, Lily Danek. Off we headed for California flying the race route backward. The planes were handicapped according to make and speed. I was flying my Cessna 172. It served me well. We were allowed four days to cross the country with no flying after day light hours. I think I remember coming in second in my category. That was a long way from the first over all. But it was fun.

My main races were the Indiana races. It was not a speed race it was a precision race. It was a race of approximately 250 miles. The planes were impounded the night before the race. Then we were told where the race was to be. With four pylons anywhere across Indiana, we learned our great State. I flew these races for several years and was very proud of my results. We had to guess our speed and fuel the night before the race and then the one coming closest to their own estimation was the winner. I was proud of my racing achievements. Many times I came in second but alas, never first. I made second many times, third and fourth and that was pretty good out of about 33 planes. My copilot was Jo Jackson. We had a lot of fun. There came times when we didn't care if we won, but we wanted to beat her husband, my formal flying instruction. He was flying with another man. I told you this was a fun race.

But I have to tell you about the one that was the most fun of all. We came in last. The race started in Seymour that day. After the planes were impounded we were given the race route. It was from Seymour, to Green Castle, to Washington, to a grass strip down on the Ohio and back to Seymour. I was very happy when they gave us the route. I had just flown a man the day before from Seymour to Green Castle for a golf game. I knew the way, I thought. It was hazy and I missed the Green Castle airport. I had to circle to find it. Then I flew along the runway at four hundred feet to be checked out by the timers on the ground. Many precious minutes and estimated fuel consumption were lost.

But then on we went to the next pylon at Washington, Indiana. I knew we had a strong wind from the West so I corrected for the wind. Did I correct too much? I looked down and we were crossing a four lane road and I did recognize it. The only four lane road in this area was St. Rd. 41 from Terre Haute to Evansville. We were in Illinois. I know Jo and I were laughing this whole trip. More time and fuel lost and now to find Washington. It had no navigational aid and we were guessing. We flew around several towns to see if we could find a water tower with a name. Did I say we were experienced pilots? We found the runway at Washington and flew across the pylon. Then I radioed Seymour to save supper for us, "we would be in sometime'. Now, on to the Ohio River we flew. I do not know how we found the runway that was only a farmer's field, but we did find an air plane parked at the edge of a grass field and flew the pylon and then on to Seymour. I can truthfully say we had more fun on this race than any other. We did it.

Jo's husband was not flying this race, he was waiting for us. I don't remember what he said. Maybe I don't want to know what he was thinking. Yes, flying can be fun. We came in last, but we got there.

My flying has taken me from the Pacific Ocean to the Atlanta Ocean, from Alaska to Florida and many places in between. My flying friends have become a big part of my life. They are a wonderful group of women and men.

I was able to fly the length of the Grand Canyon. In later years I was to take my Granddaughters and raft through the bottom of that Canyon.

Chapter 68 —
Lightening

I COULD SEE THE black storm clouds in the west. They didn't look very far away. I was at the Bedford airport getting ready to head for my home base in Indianapolis. My baby, the Cessna 172 airplane, was gassed up and ready to go. My talk to the controllers at Indianapolis Flight Service assured me if I left immediately I would miss the storms. My flight plan was filed.

"Come on, Frank" I said to my passenger. "The controller said if we hurry we will miss the storm."

As we hurried to the airplane and settled into our seats, I looked at those black and grey clouds looming above is. But the controller said it was OK. Hurrying to the end of the runway and keeping an eye on those threatening clouds, I begin to have my doubts. After a very quick run up, I headed my Baby down run way 32. She was a good old bird and lifted off in her usual smooth manner. I talked to the controller and activated my flight plan. My heading was to the north east toward Indianapolis and then all Thunder broke loose. The dark sky became black. I reached for the red night light so I could see my instruments. The plane had a special red light so airplane instruments can be read in the dark and dark it was. It was dark until the lightening flashed. Then it was blinding. The lighting was all around us and the rain came down. Carburetor heat was pulled on to keep the engine from icing up. The noise of the thunder was deafening. The plane rocked with the fury of the storm. How wrong can the controller be? We were in constant contact with each other. He asked me what I could see. I told him only blackness and a lot lighting flashes. Then he asked me if it was all right to send me across the restricted area of Atterbury. Was he crazy? I don't care where he sends me; just get me out of this storm. The seat belts were straining as the plane was shoved from one side to the other. The lightening flashes would temporary blind a person and then the eyes would adjust and I could read the instruments again. Keep my altitude was first in my mind. Don't let the plane lose its height. Those wings have to be keep as level as possible. I do not want the wing to get low and I would lose control,

What seemed like a long time and I am sure it was not nearly as long as it seemed, I could see the clearing up ahead. It was a welcome sight. The evening sky was getting dark and the ground lights were beginning to sparkle in the distance. In this section of the sky the stars were out. Behind me it was all black. The ground lights and the sky lights mingled together and again the instruments had to be read to see which part of the plane was up. Soon this section of the earth would be covered with the black monster behind me. But now, I was in friendly territory and would soon be at my home base of Post Air in Indianapolis. God was leading me home and safe again.

Chapter 69 —
Hitchhiker and the Voice

THE TELEPHONE RANG. THE voice was asking if he could hitch hike a ride from Indianapolis to Wichita Falls, Texas. My plans were to fly Eddie Wilson to see her daughter in the hospital. The daughter, Val, was in the Air force. The plans were all made to fly my Cessna 172. The flight plans were all complete. I was leaving at six the next morning. I told the man of my plans and if he wanted to go, the back seat would be empty and he was welcome to ride along. He was there when we were ready to take off. This man had never been in an airplane before, neither a big plane nor a small private plane. He had no inkling of what would happen on this flight.

The flight was uneventful until we were over Missouri. Then nature let go with one of its mighty rages and furies. The sky became black, with flashes of white hot lighting shooting in all directions. The winds were wild not knowing where they were coming from or where they were going. The little airplane was doing its best to ride it out. I was doing my best to keep the wings level. The plane was being thrown up and down, side ways and all directions in between. The seat belts were being tested as our weight was thrown against them. I knew if I let a wing down it would pitch beyond my control. I turned the night light on, but the red glow did not help in reading the instruments. They were rotating completely out of the norm. I was supposed to be in Kansas City control, but there was no radio contact. I keep calling "Kansas City this in Cessna 19773, Kansas City this is Cessna 19773. Come in. Come in Kansas City". No answer. Everything was silent from the radios. Only the howling wind and the crashing lighting could be heard. My passengers never said a word. The strain on my whole body, trying to keep the plane upright, was terrific.

I kept calling, "Kansas City, this is Cessna 19773". No response. Then came a beautiful loud and clear voice. "I CAN RELAY YOUR MESSAGE TO KANSAS CITY". The voice came back and said,

"KANSAS CITY SAYS TO TAKE A HEADING OF 270 DEGREES". Later, I asked the others if they heard that voice. No one heard it except me. Oh, what a beautiful voice.

The one instrument that was working was the manual stand by compass. I changed directions to 270 degrees and with in minutes we were out of the storm. God was leading me directly to Wiley Post Airport in Oklahoma City. I landed using the Vasi lights. These are lights set up to guide an airplane into a safe landing. Without radios and visual contact, a pilot looks for the lights on both sides of the runway. If the lights showed up red that means that the aircraft is to low. If the lights showed up white that means the aircraft is too high. If the pilot can see a little of both lights, red and white, that means he or she is on the glide path. The good little plane came in doing what it is supposed to do. Prayers brought the plane to a good landing. But there was a terrific wind coming from all directions. The people at the airport met my airplane on the runway and walked me back to the ramp. The men held on to the wings so the very strong wind would not turn me over. In a strong wind, with the power reduced an airplane can act like a kite and do what the wind wants it to. The airport knew I was coming. That is the wonders of radar. Kansas City was able to track me and tell Wiley Post Airport I was coming. The men were waiting to walk my plane to a safe tie down.

It was after we were out of the plane that the people told us we had been flying in a tornado. The hitchhiker said he knew something was wrong when he saw all the instruments going around and around. Then he left and disappeared. I never saw him again. I wonder what he is now telling his grandchildren. Is he mentioning the storm and that crazy woman pilot? Is he talking about his experience of flying in the tornado? Did he get to Texas?

The storm continued for the next two days. Eddie went on to Texas by bus, I stayed in Oklahoma City with the airplane until the storm was over and then I flew my plane on to Texas. The radios were still having problems, sometimes they would work and some times they would not. I did not know what was wrong with them until later when my mechanic had more time to check them out. The ground wires had been broken off in the storm. That is the reason for no radio contact.

I went into the Air Force airport at Wichita Fall, Texas and they knew I was having trouble communicating. I was given the lights in the tower to tell me when to land and when not to land. The green lights meant it was safe to land. The red lights say to circle again. There were other variations, but that is the main idea. I had no trouble. I stayed a few days with Eddie and her daughter. Then we headed home. With the lack of radios we struck out for a straight line to Indianapolis, Ind. We did not fly into the large airports. We landed in only the small air fields because of no communication.

I still wonder what the hitchhiker remembers about his first trip in an airplane.

Where did that voice come from that stormy night when the radios were not working? Who was that voice? I know. It had to be a voice from Heaven.

Chapter 70 —
Flying the Alcan to Alaska

WHY? MY EXCUSE WAS to attend the 99 International Convention of Women Pilots in Anchorage, Alaska. The real reason was to fly the Alcan Highway. It is the ultimate. Can you imagine reliving history? I flew over and looked down on the little ribbon of a road that our two countries, United States and Canada, made in nine months, fifteen hundred miles through the wilderness and mountains of Canada. What a feat.

WHEN? July 26, 1984 to August 19, 1984

HOW MANY PEOPLE? Two. For almost two years, I knew I was going. I had been looking around for a co-pilot. Not just anyone would do. I had to have someone whom I liked, who could fly every other leg, was easy to get along with, who enjoyed life and adventure, because this was going to be a fun trip. I picked Glory VanArsdel. I didn't know her well, but it was a very wise choice. I am sure our friendship has been bonded for life. She is a beautiful woman, both inside and out. We could both see the wonders of this earth. We are fortunate God gave us eyes to view these wonderful sights.

AIRCRAFT? My baby, a Cessna 172. She is of a 1972 vintage. I am in love with a hunk of metal.

WHAT STOPS? These are magical names of the towns were we stopped, Cedar Rapids, Iowa; Sioux Falls, Mitchell, Pierre in South Dakota; Miles City, Lewistown, Cut Bank in Montana; Lethbridge, Calgary, Edmonton, Grand Prairie in Alberta, Canada; St. John, Fort Nelson in British Columbia, Watson Lake and Whitehorse in the Yukon. Then we went to Skagway by car. Finally we went through customs at Northway into Alaska. We were stopped by weather and stayed in Gulkana, Alaska before we could go on into Anchorage.

Coming back, we went a more straight route. We flew the Alcan and then cut across Canada to Whitecourt, Wainwright and Regina. We came into customs at Minot, North Dakota, on to Aberdeen, Sioux Falls, Cedar Rapids and home to Indianapolis.

WEATHER? Although I am Instrument rated, this trip was to be only VFR (Visual Flight Rules). We were going to take our time and if the weather was bad, we were going to enjoy the people we met on the ground. Delightful!

BEFORE FIRST ALCAN FLIGT. Alcan stands for Alaska and Canadian road. Preparations were to take many months. There were maps to be bought (over $100 worth), information about flying in another country, information about flying across wilderness, plane to get ready and collecting camping gear.

The back seat of the plane was taken out to make room for our equipment. Every thing had to be weighed. We must not go over the limit for my plane. We did not weigh out purses. Do you think that would put us overweight? We stored survival gear in every pocket of our clothing and every crevice of the airplane.

It was required by Canada, that if we were to fly over the wilderness we had to have a gun with us. Alaska would allow us to have a handgun, but in Canada we had to have a long barrel gun. A friend loaned us an "over under 22 and 440". We practiced with both the rifle and the shotgun. This gun was in case we were forced down in the wilderness. We were also warned it was not for shooting bear. It was for food only. The gun would not kill a bear it would only make them angry. We had to have many different kinds of signaling devices. The airplane had an ELT (Emergency Locating Transmitter). We also had a hand held ELT. One bedroll was bright orange so it could be seen from the air. We had mirrors for signaling. Fishing tackle and a 50 foot rope were required as well as emergency food and medication. The fifty foot rope was for climbing the rough terrain and storing foot across trees to keep bears from getting to it.

Unusual? Of course. I am spoiled. I live in that part of the country where we have the agonic line of 0 degrees, meaning the compass heading is true north. . The isogonics line is the imaginary line that shows the points of the earth having the same magnetic variation from true north. Near Lewistown, Montana the compass heading is 19 degrees East from true north. Between Miles City and Lewistown, we flew north to skirt a thunderstorm. We came back to our original plan by flying 180 degrees. We did not take into consideration 19 degrees East. Do you think we would have ended up in Florida, if we had had enough fuel? Coming to out senses??????, we began to follow a road. Oh, what wonderful and desolate scenery. I realized we should be flying between two mountains. To our left, we had nothing by a big wide western plain. The mountain to our right was Big Snowy Mountain. We should have been on the other side of it. So, we just circled Big Snowy and came to our destination from the opposite directions. Even flight service was calling us before we contacted them. Our sister plane with Betty and Curt DeBaun had been in Lewistown for at least an hour before we came in. They were worried. But, as I explained, we were not lost. "We only wanted to see what was on the other side of the mountain".

Smelling fuel in the air can be frightening. Glory and I did not want to frighten the other one, so we said nothing to each other about smelling gas as we winged our way from Cutbank to Calgary for Canadian Customs. But as we flew over Lethbridge, we could not keep silent any longer. We radioed for permission to go through customs on Sunday morning at their little airport.

. It was pouring rain and we had to stay in the plane until the custom man could come from church. All the people tried to help us find the gas leak. Everything was taken out of the airplane. This was considerable because the back seat had been taken out to make room for our camping equipment. We did not find the cause for the gas smell, but we did find another disaster. Everything was wet. Even our 22/440, (over under) gun that we carried as part of our survival equipment was wet. Our wet baggage was due to our water supply that was not pressurized.

On we went—still smelling gas. Edmonton Tower wanted to know if we were the plane that was having trouble. Our problem had preceded us. I put my "baby" in maintenance and the mechanics came up with the idea that the gasket on the right wing tank was leaking. We left Edmonton with the happy feeling that our gas problem was solved. No—that smell was still with us. Even with the smell, we were enjoying the beautiful colors of the earth. The colors of the earth were many, many shades of green. It was spectacular. Everywhere we looked we could see a different color. I did not know there were that many shades of green.

The weather caught us a Ft. Nelson and we went into town for a motel and laundry mat. When we saw the inches of mud on the vehicles traveling the Alcan, we were happy to be flying the air road.

The rain was still coming down the next day. These kind people let me put my plane in an empty WWII hanger. Again everything was taken out and dried. My prop had been used for a clothesline many times. A number of stranded 99s congregated in the hanger for lunch. We were happy to lighten our load of to much survival food.

Glory was flying the next leg into Watson Lake. As we came over the lake and looked at the "little bit of Land" that extends out to form the runway, Glory said, "Ooooh Boooy!" That said it all.

The two planes left Watson Lake for Whitehorse. The landing lights were on. The valley did not seem wide enough for two planes to pass. We just wanted to be sure we were at a different altitude than the landing lights we might see coming toward us. The sides of the mountains looked like I could reach out and touch them. Rain began to fall, visibility went down. Soon I could not see the side of the mountain. I was trying to keep the plane over that white ribbon of a road. Surely the mountains would not be over the road. Betty Debaun in the lead plane radioed back that they were turning around. I said we would follow as soon as I could find a valley big enough for me to make a turn. Swan Lake was the answer. We turned back and out ran the storm back to Watson Lake. This was a camping night between the runway and the lake. Our tents went up and supper was over before the storm hit.

We were snug in out sleeping bag cocoons in our tent. Glory and I went to sleep and just let it rain. Curt with Betty in the other tent said he did not sleep well. He heard bears, wolves, loons, and Nellie snoring— Me? He shouldn't let a little think like that kept him from a good night's sleep. The next morning after breakfast there was time to pick some wild strawberries. Luscious! We had been tied down in a big wild strawberry patch. Strawberries never tasted so good.

My plane was parked with the right wing slightly lower that the other one. The right side of the airplane was completely covered with red dye. I was burning 80 octane gasoline which is colored with red dye. The gas smell was not our imagination. The next stop with maintenances was Whitehorse. The airplane "hospital' was going to find out what was wrong.

We left the plane in Whitehorse maintenances and rented a car to drive to Skagway. Skagway is in Alaska and on the coast of the Inter passage. What a wonderful side trip. The road was rough. Big boulders were in the center of the supposed to be road. It took a lot of skill to dodge the big rocks and keep the car going the directions we wanted it to go. We were told when we rented the car not to worry if the windshield would come back with cracks. It was expected as the rocks flew from the road by passing cars. It was a thrill to cover the same territory the Klondike Gold rushers covered in 1898. I even tried panning for gold. It took about one half hour to find 3 or 4 flakes of the shinny stuff. That is hard work, even if the gold was guaranteed. I believe I could make more money washing dishes.

Did you know there is a desert in the Yukon? It is a true desert with desert plants. The earth has its own secrets. Rain does not get to this spot of the earth. It is a beautiful spot.

The airport at Skagway was very interesting. One end of the runway terminates with the water in the bay, the other three sides are mountains. Can you imagine landing on a runway of 3400 feet with three windsocks, one at each end and one in the middle, all saying the wind is coming from a different directions? The narrow gage railroad that was built in about 1898 held a fascination for me. The track was laid on land that was cut out of the side of the mountain, what a feat of engineering. The train was not running at this time. But I was very much interested in that railroad. A few years later when it started up as a tourist attraction, I had to go back just to take the ride over the mountains from Skagway to Whitehorse. History is exciting.

My plane is finally fixed. The wing on top of the gas tank was taken off. The spout was cracked halfway around, the tank had a break of about four inches. The tank was emptied, cleaned, welded, put back in and refueled. We were thankful nothing more serious had happened. This had to happen in Cutbank when the weather was below freezing. The Line Boy had to climb a ladder to put the gas nozzle in the top of the wing. He evidently slipped and pulled the gas nozzle and cracked the gas tank. We had smelled gasoline every since we had left the lower 48 states.

Alaska was next. Northway, here we come. I am sure Customs sensed our elation at being in the far North. Also we did not smell gasoline on this last leg.

Weather was keeping us from going on into Anchorage. Glory and I were camping at Gulkana, Alaska. This is Glory's birthday. What more could a girl want? She is camping out at the foot of a beautiful snow capped mountain. God's flower garden is the wild flowers at the side of the runway. Alaska has more wild flowers than any other country on this earth. The evening sun gave the whole scene a rosy glow. Beautiful!! Her birthday dinner was special, canned shrimp with sauce, Dinty Moore Stew with a side dish of beets. Dessert was a-la- crumb cookie. Our tent was pitched on gravel, but we slept the "sleep of the innocent". Glory said, "That proves we are not princesses". This place had a chemical pilots lounge. That is better than going off into the trees with a shovel.

Although the next morning was bright and sunny in Gulkanna, we couldn't get through Tahneta Pass on our way to Anchorage. By noon the ceiling was three thousand feet and we were given the go ahead. We could see this layer of clouds settled in the valley. We dived down to go under them, to find a small mountain immediately in front of us. Following the road we banked to the right, then straight ahead until the road begins to climb into the clouds. We take the river valley and caught the road a short distance ahead. We come upon the beautiful

Matanuska Glacier. No thrill ride in an amusement park could equal what we experienced.

We contacted Anchorage Control and were told to stay between the road and the mountain. The road was built on the mountain. Just how were we supposed to do that? The other side of the road was a restricted area. Landing lights are on so planes in the opposite directions could see and avoid. Anchorage Control has six big airports to watch over. . They do a beautiful job. I was turned over to Merrill Tower. He told me I was second to land following a Cherokees. As I looked up, the Cherokee is coming from my left and going behind me. I asked the tower if he wanted me to make a 360 and said he would appreciate it. The controllers are so calm that it helps to make every one else calm.

We had another side trip to a wilderness camp in a Beaver airplane on floats. The trip was highlighted by the sighting of many moose. The pilot was kind enough to circle many of these animals. He would put the airplane up on a wing and turn around the animal. He said since we were all pilots we wouldn't mind. Two of us were pilots in that plane, but two were not. When the pilot found out that two were inexperienced flyers, he said he wouldn't do that again. This pilot landed in swamp area and the touch down was so smooth that hardly a ripple was made in the grassy water. I am sure some of the best pilots in the world live in Alaska.

Our adventure continues as we winged our way toward home. As we were nearing the border from Alaska into Canada, what a surprise we got. This was the middle of August, but that didn't mean anything to the weather. What is that white stuff coming down? Whoever is in charge of the weather was giving us a snow shower so we would remember the North County. It lasted for some time, but visibility was fair and we had no trouble getting into Whitehorse.

On the way home, at Watson Lake, we took time to see the famous Mile Post. It would not be a completed trip unless one can see all the signs people have carried from all over the world to post in this spot. It was started by some lonely people that were working on the Alcan Highway. They put up a sign saying how many miles it was to their hometown. Since then, many hundreds of poles and signs have told the story of "how many miles to back home". There was even a sign saying how many miles to Bedford, Indiana.

At Liard River between Watson Lake and Fort Nelson, we spotted a large forest fire with smoke drifting down the valley we intended to travel. We reported it to Flight Service at Watson Lake. They asked several questions, such as which way the smoke tower was leaning, etc. I am sure firefighting tankers were sent immediately. These airplanes were on all the fields and were always in use. We did see a number of forest fires. This was a "low " as we are thinking of all the beautiful things being destroyed. It was a "high" thinking of all the things our eyes did see. Nothing could dampen our spirits, not even the gasoline smell.

It is true the closer to home, the straighter our path took. When we left Whitecourt, we cut straight across the middle of Canada. We came thought U.S. Customs at Minot, N. D. A short time after leaving Minot my artificial horizon was telling me I was flying sideways. It was a beautiful day and I knew better. The vacuum pump had given up. I was not going to fly at night. I continued on. I did not think that instrument was going to bother me. But it wasn't long until I couldn't stand those diagonal lines. I slapped a piece of paper over its face. No problem after that.

There was excitement seeing our home base. There was sadness knowing our great adventure was over. I had picked the perfect partner and things went well. We had flown the Alcan Highway into Alaska.

WE DID IT WE DID IT WE DID IT

Chapter 71 —
God is Always With Me

GOD HAS ALWAYS BEEN with me. Here is more proof. I had just dropped my granddaughters off at Ball State University in Muncie, Indiana and was flying back to Bedford, Indiana and enjoying the beautiful countryside. One of my joys of owning my own airplane is being able to fly and to see this earth from above. I like to watch the patches of color as if a huge quilt blanketed the earth. This happens in all seasons. The spring brings its many shades of green, sprinkled with dots of color from red bud and dogwood. The summer is full of exciting and intense feelings of light. Autumn is ablaze with the artist pallet of paint before it goes to sleep for the winter. Even winter has a quilt of many, many colors of browns. All of it is beautiful.

As usual the sound of the humming engine of Cessna 172 number 19773 was music to my ears. It had never purred as gentle and as sweet as it had that day for the trip from Muncie to Bedford. No wonder I caller her 'MY BABY".

That night I stayed at my Dad's in Bedford and then was off for the airport the next morning, headed for Cedar Rapids, Iowa to visit my son, Randy and family.

The morning was overcast and the ceiling was about 1200 feet. No problem. I am instrument rated and had no trouble keeping current. I flew several times a week in most kinds of weather. I did have some weather such as storms, ice, severe wind that I did not intend to transgress. But conditions are unpredictable. One has to be ready for anything.

This morning there was only clouds. No problem. As a good instrument pilot, I called from the ground to get clearance and weather before taking off. The plane had been gassed up the night before and after the walk around checklist, every thing was 'go'.

The wind favored runway 32. At about 1000 feet, the microphone was in my hand to call Indianapolis and ask for permission to go into the clouds and climb to whatever altitude I have been give on my telephone briefing. The engine became very rough. Not only the engine, the whole plane seemed to shake like a big dog had picked it up in its teeth and was trying to kill what every wild animal it had just caught. I certainly could not go into the clouds with 'my baby' acting like that.

I told you God was always with me. This was His way of warning me of things to come. I turned back toward the Bedford Airport. Then the unthinkable happened. Every thing went silent. The engine had quit and only the sound of the propeller as it was winding down could be heard. My knees begin to knock together. They were hitting hard enough that it was hurting. I think that must have been one of the ways to keep my mind off what was happening. Taking one hand, I hit one knee as hard as I could and told them to be still. They minded me and behaved like a child that had been punished.

Calling the airport Unicom with the information of what was happening, I told them I was coming in on runway number 6. Of course every one at the airport met my plane as it glided to a stop.

I asked the airport manager, Ralph Rogers, if my voice had betrayed me when I called in on the radio. He said "No", but my hands sure did when I stepped out of the airplane. God had warned me to turn back before I lost gliding distance of the airport. Yes, He has always been with me.

The engine was torn down to check what had gone wrong. Nothing was found, except that both sparkplugs on the same cylinder had fouled out. That would have made the engine rough, but would not have necessarily killed it. No reason was every found for why the engine quit. Maybe it was bad gas. Whatever the reason, God had warned me to turn back and I had listened to Him.

Chapter 72 —
Time to Say Goodbye

IT IS TIME TO say "good bye". Tears were close to the surface. I must not cry, but she had been a good part of my life for almost twenty years. We had gone through so much together and she had never failed me. I loved her and I called her, "My Baby". To some she might be only a hunk of metal, called an airplane. But to me she was part of my life.

She had carried me from Alaska to Florida and from the Pacific to the Atlantic and many places in between. She was a 1972 Cessna 172 airplane. I bought her sight unseen. I bought her in 1974. I had heard about her sitting in a field in Kentucky. She had belonged to a construction company which had gone bankrupt. They had left her sitting in a field all alone with no one to take care of her. When she arrived in Columbus, Indiana she had been used only 117 hours. She was almost new, but her brakes were slightly rusted from being left in the field all alone. The problem could be solved easily by my mechanic.

I had my pilot's license when my husband died in December 1972. We owned a Cessna 150, a two place airplane. Within two weeks after his death I had gone into instrument training. It was something I wanted and I knew I would have to work hard to get my Instrument license. I would not have time to feel sorry for myself. I was very thankful to have a good job. I was the Food Director of Warren Township Schools on the east side of Indianapolis, Indiana. For the next year I worked hard in my little Cessna 150 on my Instrument training. But there came a time when I needed something bigger and with more advanced avionics. That is when "My Baby" came to me.

I got my instrument license in 1974 and from that time forward we were almost inseparable. Almost every afternoon after school, I would head for the field where I kept "My Baby". We would fly together. Much of the time would be practicing take off and landings. She knew what I wanted and I knew what she wanted and we worked together. I was proud of her. We flew the skies together. Sometimes we would spot a cloud and we would dive for it just to see the cloud dissipate as the heat of the engine evaporated the little cloud. There were times we just flew over the fields and watched the colors change with the seasons. We would follow the rivers. We even flew the length of the Grand Canyon. What a thrill. We flew through two mountains in the Yukon and the mountains looked close enough that a wing could touch the side.

Even when I got bad gasoline, the plane with God's help brought me back to the airport safely, even when the motor had stopped.

My Baby and I went through a tornado over Oklahoma. The ride was very rough and the wind was fierce. I was fighting to keep the wings lever so it would not pitch out of control. The plane minded me and again with God's help we came out of it. We even had a Heavenly Voice come in the cabin telling us which direction we should go to get out of the storm.

I am a short person and I had to have a footstool to get into my own airplane. It was a little stool and I had it tied to a rope. Once I was in the airplane, I could pull it up inside the plane and I would have it for the next time. There was a time when I forgot to pull it up and as I was taxing down the runway, I heard something banging on the side of the plane. I had to stop and bring my little footstool inside with me. Oh yes, my baby and I have had a lot of experiences.

We have raced against other planes. The Powder Puff Derby was a speed race from California to Delaware.

One race I entered every year was a precision race. It was the one I enjoyed most. It was "Know Your Own Airplane" I did know my own airplane. She was a joy to fly.

Now it was time to say, "Good Bye". In the last year I had her, I only used her for 35 hours; that is not enough practice for my ability to stay good. She deserved someone that would fly her and treat her kindly; the year before that she was used only 50 hours. In earlier times I would put between 200 and 300 hours on her a year. Yes, it was time to say, Good Bye

I had sold her and I was now taking her for my last good bye flight. I talked to the controllers as I left the airport and told them I had sold the airplane and I was just taking her for my last flight to say good-bye to her. The controllers knew me; because I flew a lot; I only knew them by their voices. They had even wished me a safe trip when I had left for California to fly in the Power Puff Derby. Now they said they would watch out for me and I was to go and enjoy my flight. I took that airplane as high as it would go. We went almost 15,000 feet. The plane was still climbing slowly, but I was not. I did not have extra oxygen. It was time to get closer to the ground. Then I would dive down and do all kinds of maneuvers. I was just having fun. I think the little plane enjoyed it, also.

After about an hour it was time to bring her in. We did a nice soft landing and taxied to the tie down spot. I stepped out and locked the door. I wanted to put my short arms around her and to say good- bye, but I was to near tears. I walked away and did not look back. I put the keys in the office for the next owner and walked to my car. I did not dare look toward her as I drove away from the airport. Yes, it was time to say "Good- Bye", but "Good- Byes" are not always easy. However, good memories will last forever.

Part Thirteen:
GROWING OLDER

Chapter 73 —
Things I want to know

THINGS I WOULD LIKE to know about old age. I have reached that time and I am curious. I try to do the things I am supposed to, but I know my body is getting older. I have reached ninety years.

I exercise three times a week at Water aerobics. I try to eat right. That doesn't mean I always do it. My snacks are walnuts.

I know I have arthritis in my hands. What is arthritis? I know it is inflammation of the joints, but it is also a build up of something. What is that something? My fingers are larger at the joints. One finger catches and then pops as I try to move it. I suppose it is all over my body, but that is the only place I have pain and notice it.

Why, since I exercise, do my wrist and ankle want to "give away with me" at times. Not all the time. But some time they are weaker than I want them to be.

I am still able to walk, drive a car and work on my pencil drawings. My art work is a big part of my life.

The most important part of my life is my work on Teddy Bears. I have been doing that for almost twenty years. There are about six of us at church and we work every Wednesday morning making these teddy bears to give to the children in the hospitals or any where else a little teddy bear can help a child. We make about four hundred and fifty teddy bears a year.

Does Neuropathy have a tendency to be heredity? I look back on my family, and it seems to me there was a lot of it. My two sons, age 70 and 65 have been diagnosed with it. I think my dad had some. He could fall and stumble at times. His dad, my grandfather, was very unsteady as he tried to walk and there came a time he couldn't walk and he was only 78 when he died. Of course my dad was 92. I am coming up on that. I am now 90. My brother also has it and has given up driving because of numbness in his feet. Sometime my feet feel like they have an extra sole on the bottom. However, they are not numb.

Although I have all of these questions, I feel I am very fortunate to be able to get around and do the things I do. Even my Neuropathy is better. I say better because I can walk more in the grocery store and not hurt. I can stand a little longer than I use to. I can not walk on uneven ground at all. I use a walking stick if I want to go out into the yard.

Chapter 74 —
Senior Citizen Dance

THE GENTLEMAN ASKED ME if I would like to go to the Senior Citizen Dance. Me, an eighty eight year old gal said, "Sure". He told me I would see a lot of people I knew. He did not dance, but he liked to listen to the music.

He was right, I did see a lot of people I knew and the music was the kind of music l liked when I was younger. But he couldn't begin to imagine what I would discover.

We were sitting near the band, Merle Cox and Friends, and the place vibrated with the beat of the music. Our table was rocking. Those sitting next to me were beating the table like it was a drum. Not only that, but the so called senior citizens on the dance floor were dancing and swaying to the beat of the music. Their faces were smiling or laughing as the music moved them. They were having a great time and I am sure they were not thinking or any problems they left behind them as they came to this Senior Citizen Dance. The floor was crowded at every dance. The band would play a slow piece and then a fast piece. The roster said there were 138 people there that night and most of them were on the dance floor. The floor was crowded at every dance. They may not be eligible for "Dancing With The Stars", but who cares? They were having a good time.

There was the little woman that had a lot of wrinkles in her face and her hair was white. She had a jewel encrusted tiara crowning that pretty white hair and her eyes sparkled with the rhythm of the music. Her feet wore corrective shoes and her four prong cane had a flower bouquet at the handle. Her party dress was ruffled at the bottom. Many men asked her to dance. She could leave her cane and depend upon the men to hold her as they danced. If she didn't have a partner she would stand in front of the band and keep her feet moving while she held on the cane. But she had a partner most of the time.

There was the man that came through the door and was barely able to shuffle his feet. But there on the dance floor, he could shuffle his feet with the music. He would pick a partner and shuffle around the floor.

There were people of all shapes and sizes. Some were tall and big, but they could make their bodies twist to the music and the partners would do the same. Even the big ones could twist their torso in the imitation of the hula.

Jeans were the dress of the night. But many of the men had their jeans belted with beautiful leather embedded with silver emblems.

There was the gentleman who wore suspenders to hold up his pants. They were necessary because his middle extended over his belt area. But his eyes were sparkling as he danced to the music. No one cared how old the person was or what shape age had left their bodies in. It was the beat of the music and the smiles on their faces that counted. Exercise is good for the brain. Their brains were being nurtured. Hugs were plentiful and there were plenty of them to go around. As one partner would whisper to another on the dance floor, laughter would ring out and the beat kept on going.

What a blessing this Senior Dance place is. It has taken a lot of work to make it special. Mary Guthrie, who is the head of the Senior citizens in Mitchell, Indiana, has worked hard to make a goal of this unusual place. It is a wonderful thing for these people that will not allow them to think of their age. The smiles on their faces and the sparkle in their eyes tell it all. You people out there that have not given this place a try come and join in the fun. It is held every Friday and Saturday night at the Senior Citizen building in Mitchell, Indiana. Dinner is three dollars and some of the people pitch in with all kinds of wonderful things to eat. .

Chapter 75 —
Can you Guess?

THE LADY RECEIVED A telephone call from a gentleman. The man asked her if she wanted to go to the airport with him for "Old Timers Meeting"

The lady said "Of course I will go with you.'

The gentleman said he would be over after her in about an hour. They both hung up the receiver.

Then the woman though "Oh no, I just took a water pill. Well, I told him I would go, so I will just have to make the best of it"

In an hour the car pulled up and the lady got into the car and they headed for the airport.

Then the gentleman started to apologize to the lady. "I am sorry; I took a water pill this morning."

The conversation turned to their ailments.

Can you guess the age bracket of this couple?

Chapter 76 —
Splinters

THE WARM SUN WAS shinning. The waves from the Gulf of Mexico were lapping at the white sand. It was a wonderful day to walk the beach. The way from the condo to the beach was an old wooden walkway. It had weathered many storms and the wood was dried and splintery. Many times I have taken hold of the wooden rails to steady myself and splinters would get in my hand. This time I would protect myself and wear light weight gloves to hold onto the wooden rail.

It worked. I got to the end of the walkway and was ready to step onto the beautiful white sand. A friend met me as he was coming into the walk way from the beach. We were talking and I leaned next to the wooden fence. Where do you suppose I got the splinter? You are right. The splinter went right into my rear end. I pulled the big part out and then went back to the condo for my daughter-in-law to pull the rest of it out. It had not gone into my skin, but I could feel the sharp point. It was imbedded into my clothing

Splinters come in all shape and sizes. They come from anywhere and can get anywhere. Beware.

Chapter 77 —
Happy Snake

IT WAS SPRING. How wonderful after the cold and windy days of winter. The birds were singing and even the animals had a smile on their faces.

I was feeling the elations that comes with the magic of spring. Walking around the cabin that was near the Nation Forest I enjoyed each young sprig that was coming through the ground.

As I came to the corner of the cabin, I saw another happy little animal. It was a black snake. It too was enjoying the warm sunshine. It was coming across the ground in big loops. Mr. Snake would stretch out his long body across the ground them bring the tail up to the head and formed a big loop in the middle. He was in no hurry. He was just enjoying the spring day.

He did not expect to see a human at the corner and I did not expect to see a snake as I came to the corner from the opposite directions. We both stopped suddenly, I was so surprised, I did not move. He was equally surprised. He had his head up about foot off the ground and his head was facing me and he did not move. We were staring at each other. His little old black eyes were fastened on the eyes of the big human. My eyes were fastened on him.

I am so very thankful that I my grandmother taught me not to be afraid of snakes. When the grandchildren played in our grandparent's barn we were told to leave the snakes alone. They were our friends. They keep the mice and other animals from starting a fire in the barn. We were also told the difference between the faces of a poison snake and the snakes that are non poisonous.

This black snake that was starring at me was not a poisonous snake. He was an animal that helped nature keep a good balance.

We starred at each other for what seemed like a long time. I remember thinking, "Mr. Snake I am going to out stare you". I was very still and my eyes keep looking at his little black beady eyes.

I don't know how long we stood motionless, but I won. The snake all at once gave up and threw himself backward toward the cabin where there were some tall weeds. He made a big noise as his leather body hit the cabin and in seconds he was no where to be found. I am telling this story to my children and grand children. I wonder if Mr. Snake is telling the story to his off springs.

Chapter 78 —
Cat

WHAT WAS THAT TERRIBLE noise coming from the back door? "OK" I called, "I'm coming, I'm coming." I thought, " You don't have to break the house down". When I got there I was surprised to see a black and white cat climbing the screen and making the most awful noise. What could be wrong with the thing? I had never heard a cat make that kind of racket.

When I opened the screen door, he jumped down. I shooed him off the porch. He returned as soon as I closed the door to begin his attack on the house again. What could be wrong with that animal? He wanted in and I was not about to let him into my house. I did not want an animal.

He meowed, "Let me in. I want in. Give me something to eat."

I said, " I am not going to feed you and I am not going to let you in. Go home, where ever you home is".

He meowed back, " You are too. You are going to feed me or I am going to eat your house down."

"I am not."

This assault keep up for three days. Why doesn't he get tired and go back wherever he came from? I never heard of such a persistent animal. Why didn't he bother the other neighbors? Why did he pick on me? I don't need a cat. He meowed back, "you are going to take care of me".

After three days, I knew he had to be hungry. I don't want any person or animal to be hungry. So, I gave him something to eat. I put an ad in the paper for a lost cat. No response. I had me a cat or maybe I should say he had me.

He was a nice little kitty for about six months. . He was a beauty in his black and white soft fur. But he didn't have any tail. The Vet said he was born without a tail. So, I called him "Bobby". One day he was sitting on a footstool watching TV. The animal show was on and it was showing a bobcat chasing a rabbit. There after his true colors came out. He waited until he had worked his way into my heart and now he was going to show me who was boss. Whenever I walked past a door, he would jump out at me and bite my ankle. . My son said he was just showing that he loves me. Well, some way to show love! He almost lost his happy home for that. But he had already worked his way into my life. I learned to be very careful when I walked by a place he could be hiding.

He was an indoor and out door cat. He did have a litter box inside, but he preferred to use the out side. However, I couldn't understand after I put him out, why he showed up inside the house again. Then one day the mystery was solved. We were both outside and I saw him go to the screen door and sit down, put his front paws up on the door, start a slow rhythmic beat to the screen. He would get faster and faster until he got the door vibrating. Then he would take one paw and put it behind the door and flip the door open and walk in. I saw this happen many times. The intelligence of animals can be amazing.

He loved to ride in a car. I had a feeling that was the reason he got lost the first time. I lived only a few blocks from the retail mall of Washington Square in Indianapolis. I am guessing, that he got out of his owners car and for some reason could not find his way back, so he made his way to my house. My property had a long drive way. When a friend came to visit me, Bobby would meet him at the road. The car door would open and the cat would get in and ride up to the house. Bobby was king of it all.

There were many trees in my yard and of course squirrels were everywhere. He gave the squirrels a hard time, but they got even with him. When he was in the house and sitting on the window ledge looking out at his territory, the squirrel would come up to the other side of the window and put his nose up to the glass and make fun of the kitty. Bobby would go berserk. The squirrel knew Bobby couldn't get to him. The rodent wouldn't dare do that if Bobby were outside. Never underestimate the thinking of an animal. Squirrely was teasing Bobby.

I would see him go to the basement. When I went down I would look for him. He was no place to be found. I even looked up on the rafters, behind boxes, on ledges, but no Bobby. This happened for weeks. Where can that cat be hiding? Then one day as I was in the basement I saw him coming out of a box. The box was empty but the lid had been cut on three sides and the top flap folded forward to close the cardboard box. He had his own hiding place.

Bobby was with me for three and half years. The Vet said he was an old cat when he came to me. But he became a dear friend. I loved him and mourned when he died. Even though I didn't want him, I profited by his love for the length of time God gave him to me.

Chapter 79 —
What I am Thankful for

WHAT I AM THANKFUL for: There are so many things that it is hard to start.

I am thankful that God is in charge of the universe and I was brought up in a family that taught me this. I am thankful for my parents and grandparents and the way they raised me. I know that God is in charge of my life. He always has been and many times it has been proven. He has kept me from doing foolish things. When I have stepped out of line, He has always been there to pull me back. When I have gotten in trouble He has helped me get back where I belong.

I am thankful my parents taught me not to be afraid. They taught me to work my way through a lot of tough situation. If they had not taught me this, I would not have had the many experiences that have made my life richer. I was not taught to be afraid of the water. If I had been afraid, I would not have known the joy of snorkeling off the coast of Hawaii. I would not have become a swim teacher. I would not know the joy of surf boarding, or the joy of rafting through the Grand Canyon with my granddaughters. They did not tell me "don't do that you might get hurt'. I was told to be careful and use common sense. God watched out for me as He always has.

Life has been fun. Yes, there were many times things did not go as I would wish them, but He has always been with me. There was the day after my husband died. He put a little rabbit in my back yard to remind me of life. He knew that would help me go on.

When I was about eight or nine, I realized I could not sing. I wanted to sing very much. It was not to be. But God gave me a husband that had a beautiful voice. Then there came two sons that also had beautiful voices. One of them is singing with the Cedar Rapids Chorale.

If I were taught to be afraid, I would not have become a pilot and had the blessing of seeing this earth from high in the sky. I would have been afraid to try something new. I would have missed out on the joy of flying the air races, flying to Alaska, flying the mountains and making wonderful friends. When I was asked to help out in the school system at Warren Township and later became the Food Director of the whole township, I might have refused. I was able to grab what came my way. Again God made me what I am. I had the opportunity to be in the public by dancing and speaking. How wonderful I had a good speech teacher in High School.

I was thankful I had two sons that wanted to learn and that were willing to work for their education. I am thankful that by the time my husband died, the boys had their degrees and were on their own with good jobs. I am thankful for their families and my grandchildren and now the great grandchildren. I am thankful that God is in all of our lives.

I am thankful for my church and the many, many friends I have. I am thankful for my church friends, my flying friends, my work friends, my neighbor friends and my art friends. I am thankful for the group of women that make teddy bears for the children in the hospitals. If I am doing it for the children, then I am doing it for God.

I am thankful for being in this wonderful country that has allowed all of these things to come about. I am thankful for this writing class that has made me think of all of these things. I could keep on going. I don't think I would ever run out of things to be thankful for.